PECO
MODELLERS' LIBRARY

Your Guide to
MODELLING SWISS RAILWAYS
CM SWISS SPECIAL

We hope you will enjoy and be inspired by this Swiss Special, our fourth geographically-themed extra edition. The railways of Switzerland are, of course, frequently the subject of articles in CONTINENTAL MODELLER, but this Special allows us to present longer features, in more detail, and with more and larger pictures than would usually be possible in a regular issue of the magazine.

When considering what to include in this guide, we came to the conclusion that the best way to illustrate the current state of modelling Swiss railways was with the work of modellers, in Britain and on the continent. CM has a long tradition of using contributors from Europe, and several are represented here alongside 'local talent'.

In a relatively modest volume such as this, we can only hope to provide an introduction, to give a flavour, and to show something of the appeal of modelling Swiss railways. It is not such a large country, but does encompass many different landscapes, from the gently rolling country of the north and west to the alpine south and east.

We have tried to feature a mixture of scales and gauges, and layouts large and small, to cater for all tastes, and resources.

These features are supported by some prototype background and layout suggestions, and augmented with practical modelling tips.

Those interested in the railways of Switzerland are fortunate to have the support of an excellent special interest group: the Swiss Railways Society.

Due to the general lack of foreign language skills in Britain, such societies have an important rôle in translating sources of information.

The Society publishes not only a fine quarterly journal but has also produced an excellent series of booklets on specific topics. The Society and its publications are by no means restricted to modelling, and provide practical travel guides for those who wish to go and experience Swiss railways for themselves.

The railways in Switzerland have a long history, with the first line opened in 1847 between Zurich and Baden, a distance of just 16km. The network then expanded throughout the country, employing metre gauge to access mountainous areas. Swiss railways have been at the forefront of developments in railway infrastructure and technology, culminating in recent major projects to drive long, deep tunnels under the mountains.

Because the Swiss railway scene is so varied, it is difficult, and not particularly useful, to generalise about the differences between Switzerland and Britain: perhaps most obviously electrification is much more widespread, and has been for some time, due to a lack of any indigenous coal reserves to fuel steam locos and an abundance of hydro-electric schemes to provide power; there have always been significant independent as well as state railways; integrated planning and organisation of services seems to have been better managed; the recent growth of private operators is apparent in Switzerland as elsewhere in Europe; and metre gauge was widely used – and in many places still forms a very significant part of the transport system, and is not just a preserved curiosity. Preservation tends to be in the form of support groups rather than museum lines, though there are exceptions, notably the Blonay – Chamby, while the national transport museum in Luzern is superlative and SBB Historic maintains a working fleet of heritage stock.

In modelling terms, the techniques, tools, and basic materials are similar, so we have avoided covering basic ground (almost literally!). As will be seen in some of these features, some British products can be adapted.

There is no major domestic manufacturer, but there are many specialists producing high quality models, often as limited editions – names such as Fulgurex, Lemaco (now Lematec), and Hag come to mind. Major European manufacturers have of course long recognised the potential of the Swiss market, encouraged by the fact that some Swiss motive power and rolling stock can be seen beyond the borders, and stock from some other countries runs into Switzerland. As a result Swiss stock is quite well represented not only in HO (which dominates here as elsewhere) but also in Z and even more in N; TT is not common. As elsewhere, O has been on the rise in recent years, and there is also increasing interest in Gauge 1, though both remain the preserve of specialist suppliers.

Reflecting the prototype situation, certain metre gauge subjects have some commercial support, mostly in HOm, with some Om, some Nm, and a certain amount in G.

Swiss mainstream models are quite easily available from several specialist outlets in Britain, most of whom advertise regularly in CONTINENTAL MODELLER.

So, here is a selective look at Swiss railway modelling – we trust that you find it interesting and entertaining.

A brief guide to the 'Epoch/Era' dating system

As a convenient way of defining broad periods of railway history across Europe, the following terms are generally used:

EPOCH I – approximately 1870 to 1920;
vehicles in the liveries of the separate state and private railways.

EPOCH II – approximately 1920 to 1945,
from the formation of the large national state networks (DRG, BBÖ, SBB, etc).

EPOCH III – approximately 1945 to 1968.

EPOCH IV – approximately 1968 to 1994;
vehicles with UIC computer numbering.

EPOCH V – 1994 to 2006, from the foundation of DBAG,
the formation of private railway operating companies and Europe-wide liberalisation of railway traffic.

EPOCH VI – introduction of new Europe-wide UIC vehicle numbers
containing a country-specific code, starting 2007.

Scale and gauge comparison

UK		gauge (model)	Europe		gauge represented
Z	1:220	6.5mm	1:220	Z	standard
no equivalent		6.5mm	1:160	Nm	metre
N	1:148	9mm	1:160	N	standard
TT	1:100	12mm	1:120	TT	standard
OO	1:76	16.5mm	1:87	HO	standard
no equivalent		6.5mm	1:87	HOf	60cm
OO9	1:76	9mm	1:87	HOe	75/76cm
OOn3	1:76	12mm	1:87	HOm	metre
O	1:43.5	32mm	1:45	O	standard
O-16.5	1:43.5	16.5mm	1:45	Oe	75/76cm
no equivalent		22.2mm	1:45	Om	metre
1	1:32	45mm	1:32	1	standard
G	1:22.5	45mm	1:22.5	G	metre

PECO
MODELLERS' LIBRARY

Your Guide to

MODELLING SWISS RAILWAYS

CM SWISS SPECIAL

Contents

Editor	Andrew Burnham
Assistant Editor	Tim Rayner
Associate Editor & Photographer	Steve Flint
Editorial Assistant & Photographer	Craig Tiley
Art Director	Adrian Stickland
Graphic Illustration	Dave Clements, Gary Bickley, Steve Croucher
General & Advertisement Manager	John King
Direct Subscriptions	Alicia Knight
Editorial Director	Ben Arnold

ISBN 978 0 900586 58 3 **ref.PM-209**

Printed by: William Gibbons & Sons Ltd.,
P.O.Box 103, 26, Planetary Road,
Willenhall, West Midlands, WV13 3XT.

Distribution to the newsagency trade (Home & Overseas):
Marketforce (UK), Second Floor, 5, Churchill Place,
Canary Wharf, London, E14 5HU.

Somewhere on the Bern Lötschberg Simplon

Lötschbergbahn

Alison Poulter of Contikits describes her Swiss N gauge exhibition layout, set in the early 2000s and featuring a large variety of stock. *Photographs by Rebecca Flynn.*

Below
A veteran BLS Ae8/8 enjoying a day out hauling modern bogie open wagons crosses an Re10/10 combination in 'Cargo' colours with a long set of Hupac intermodal wagons loaded with trailers and swap bodies.

The inspiration for this layout came while passing many sunny afternoons in Brugg, Switzerland, watching the trains as they began the gentle ascent towards the Gotthard line. It was always a particular thrill if there was a huge rake of freight wagons as the clickety-clack was very soporific. It was this that I wanted to recreate in an exhibition layout and in essence just provide a backdrop to display the huge array of rolling stock that can be seen across Europe and especially in Switzerland.

Above
A BLS 465 with a rake of SBB EWIV coaches. On the road below work is in progress to repair damage to the surface after heavy rain caused the river to rise and flood.

My first foray into the world of railway modelling was a Swiss Z layout, *Guglingen* (CM May 2009). As I wrote at the time, I had acquired the boards with track which got me started but I was never happy with running quality. As with most exhibition layouts that I had seen then, the main problem was point failures and so I was determined to avoid having any points on the scenic side of the layout! By contrast, as I wanted continuous running of large rakes of stock, it was essential to have a sizeable fiddle yard. With this criterion in mind I set about what was to become a five year project building what is now the *Die Lötschbergbahn*. Although using artistic licence, the centrepiece of the layout is the Bietschtal bridge on the Bern – Lötschberg – Simplon line, which is one of the major routes for freight passing north to south through Europe and as such allows a huge variety of freight to be run, along with a good selection of passenger trains.

The baseboards are an L girder frame with a soft board top to keep them light. There are four 6' by 2'6" boards which fit in pairs into a carrying frame for transporting to exhibitions. There is a fixed backscene made of thin plywood.

I have used cork tiles in the fiddle yard and cork strip under the track on the scenic side for noise suppression.

The scenic side of the layout has twin tracks running over the Bietschtal bridge, which is a Faller kit. The bridge was in storage for a long time before being fitted to the layout and during this time the plastic rails along the side of the bridge became damaged. One of our customers kindly donated some etched brass railings that he had spare from a model boat (or was it a ship?!) that he had built and they give a much more realistic finish.

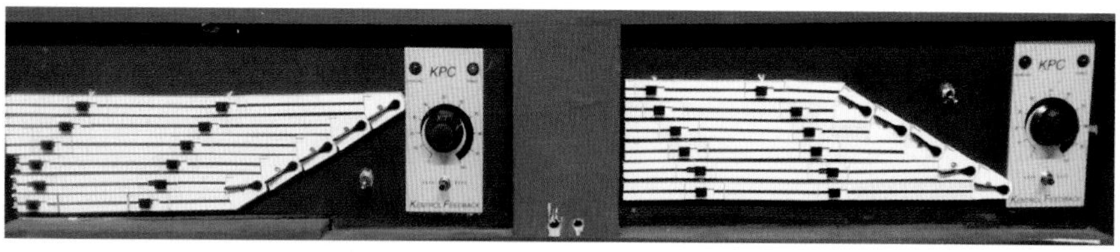

Above
Fleischmann switches were used to create a mimic board for operating the points and isolating sections.

Below
The fiddle yard always seems to be of great interest to visitors at shows.

Track

The fiddle yard consists of twelve sidings, six for each of the running lines at the front, which run the majority of the length of the layout to allow for extra long rakes of freight. The loops are between 8' and 10', which allows for long rakes of passenger coaches and freight wagons to be accommodated. They can also be split into two isolated sections for shorter freights or railcars, to increase the number of trains that can be operated in any one session.

I have used Peco code 55 flexible track with Setrack for the curves as they were a small radius and this made it easy to maintain the consistency of the curve. Peco points and point motors were used, with the point motors being mounted above the baseboards for reliability. Initially the points were operated using toggle switches but this proved confusing and unreliable so I changed to using a Fleischmann mimic board with the points wired in pairs and a capacitor discharge unit used. This has been the source of much interest at our club open days.

Below
The pastor and his wife welcome us to a location overlooking the railway.

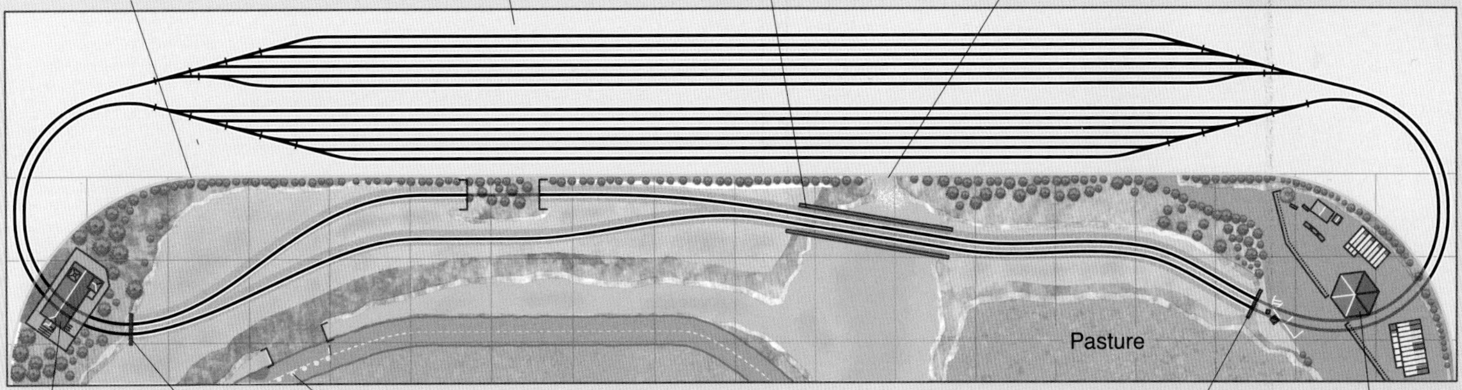

LÖTSCHBERGBAHN
Scenic size: 18' x 2' 6". Each grid square: 1ft x 1ft.

I needed to keep operation as straightforward as possible as I usually operate the layout single-handed and the visual display that the Fleischmann board gave appealed to me and seems to work. This along with two Gaugemaster panel mounted controllers allows the layout to be operated from the side. I am thus able to keep an eye on what is happening at the front and back whilst fielding the many questions that the layout and stock generate. Interestingly, what is going on in the fiddle yard often generates the greatest amount of attention!

Sommerfeldt catenary masts have been used, with brass wire between. The catenary is not currently wired for overhead running but this is a future project.

After positioning the catenary masts, the track was ready to be ballasted. This was done using Fleischmann N scale ballast which was 'sprinkled' along the track using a teaspoon. A fine mist of water was then sprayed over the track before a mixture of PVA glue and water was dropped on using a pipette. This process was repeated for any patches that were still loose. On running some locos over the track, I discovered that some of the ballast was too high so this was filed down to improve running.

Scenery

Having laid the track, the mammoth task of constructing the scenery began. As the majority of the scenery was to be rock face, I needed to get this right. I looked for advice from many people but everyone had a different approach so in the end I had to stop talking about it and just crack on with it. The form of the hillside was constructed using insulation foam. (It is worth buying the type that comes without the silver paper backing, as I spent many hours peeling this from some foam sheets I had been given!) A rough outline of the rocks was created by carving fissure lines and crevasses using a grapefruit knife. Having obtained the desired effect, the foam was covered with a thin layer of Sculptamold which was shaped to resemble the rock face. Woodland Scenics latex moulds were used to create a few feature pieces which were fixed in place using PVA glue.

Left
The 'Red Arrow' railcar on one of its many chartered special runs is entertaining the lucky guests with a champagne lunch as it passes a train of fuel tanks.

Below
An Austrian 'Railjet' on trial meets a Holcim-liveried 482 with a train of tank wagons.

The rocks were painted using a mixture of blues, greys, and white to try to recreate the colour of the rock in Switzerland.

Thin ply board was used for the backscene which was predominantly painted blue for the sky, with the impression of some mountains in the distance as you look beyond the bridge.

Small pebbles were used at the base of the waterfall and along the river bed which was also painted to create the illusion of depth. Woodland Scenics waterfall effects were used by painting thin layers onto acetates and then gluing in place using PVA. For the river, varnish was used but this was not entirely successful. Our clubrooms are by the coast and I think the salt in the air did not help because the finish was not as clear as I would have hoped. I have discovered that by rubbing the surface with a cotton wool pad and a little baby oil a more 'liquid' effect can be achieved.

On the hillside over of six hundred trees have been planted. I found the best way to buy these was in bulk packs from Germany and these often arrived within days of ordering. I was also very kindly donated some from a customer who had an excess from his own layout. The trees were positioned by drilling holes with a hand drill and gluing the trunks in place for extra security when transporting to shows. In amongst the trees you may spot some wildlife – and at our Christmas open day a Christmas tree may appear, and Santa and his sleigh can be seen in the sky above the Bietschtal bridge!

As the layout is for through running trains, there is no station or town. However, the Swiss do love their gardens, so at one end of the layout is a Faller garden centre complete with children's play area. The other end has a Vollmer church complete with a group of walkers and their dog passing by. All of the

Above
A preserved Ae4/7 meets a refurbished $Re4/4^{II}$ in Zugkraft Aargau livery.

Left
A 'rolling road' train passes a BLS 465 on an express formed with SBB coaches.

Right
An unexpected find for any rail fan – an Austrian 'Railjet' on trial is spotted by one of those having a picnic at the river's edge.

Below
The SBB Historic preserved Ae4/7 rolls the elegant *Nostalgic Orient Express* across the Bietschtal bridge and is met by an Em845 heavy shunter (a former DR V60 0-8-0) with a trip working of Hbis high capacity sliding side vans.

Above
A 460 in special advertising livery with matching coaches.

Below
The old BLS Ae8/8 passes a Hupac intermodal train of Crossrail swap bodies.

figures and animals have a pin attached to the base to hold them in place, again to avoid loss during transport to shows.

The roadworks were a more recent addition to the layout as I acquired some works vehicles with LED lights and the flashing warning bollards (made by Busch). I also have some motor cycles and bicycles with LED lights which create much interest.

Presentation

The layout sits on five builder's trestles which are light to transport and easy to assemble. The height of the layout is set a little below eye level to give the idea of viewing from a distance but still allowing children to see. There is a Perspex frontage to protect the small details from little hands!

The lighting is provided by a strip of LED lights in a flat bottom piece of guttering that is held in position by four cross braced L-shaped arms.

Stock

The period that I have chosen to model is the early 2000s through to the present day, although the occasional nostalgic train can be seen passing through. The majority of the locos are Fleischmann as the running quality and reliability of these is exceptional. Many of the Re460s are Kato or Minitrix; I have found with the latter that they need regular servicing to ensure smooth running. For the nostalgic trains I have a Roco Be4/6, a Hag Ae4/7, and the ever-popular 'Crocodile' by Arnold, along with a rake of CIWL coaches by Rivarossi and the unusual 'Red Arrow' railcar by Hobbytrain. At club open days one of the most popular trains is the set of double-deck coaches pulled by a 460 in the fictitious *Contikits on tour* livery – there is also a tour bus, containers, a lorry, and a minibus! These were created for me on the basis of three Kato sets of four Hong Kong coaches and an Re460 loco. The running quality is exceptional and I can leave this running round the layout at club open days whilst I get a much needed cuppa! Another special is the Re4/4^{II} in *Zugkraft Aargau* livery which is my favourite Swiss train as it reminds me of happy days trainspotting on the plat-

form at Brugg – this loco would go backwards and forwards all day between Aarau and Turgi. I obtained the Hag HO model and the coaches on a trip to Interlaken one year and a member of our club used this to produce waterslide transfers to convert an Arnold N model. I am still on the lookout for the coaches and driving trailer which are available in Switzerland but at a very high price.

The coaches are mainly Roco and Minitrix, although I did have some Hornby (Arnold) EWIIs but needed to change the wheelsets on these as almost all caused running problems.

I have found that many of the freight wagons are too light and I have needed to add weight to improve the running quality. The golden rule is that if it does not run well, it has no place on the layout!

Acknowledgements

I would like to take this opportunity to thank my husband Geoff for his support in this endeavour at the expense of spending time on his own layout. He introduced me to Swiss railways in 2000, along with Ernie Brack, who planned our trips with military precision.

Thanks also to Charles Duncan and Mark Knox for their electrical skills, and to Jem Soady for creating the *Zugkraft Aargau* Re4/4[II].

I am a member of the Blyth and Tyne Model Railway Society in North Shields. Being a member of this club allowed me the space to work on this layout as well as gaining knowledge and support from the other club members.

Having completed my second exhibition layout, I have already started to plan and collect the stock for my next two layouts and fully expect to have completed the third before Geoff manages to complete his 'nearly finished' Swiss O layout. The next layout was to be ÖBB Schwarzsee, Kitzbuhel, but I am awaiting the production of the diesel railcars and City Shuttle stock in N that are essential for this line. Both are available in HO but I prefer N because more realistic long rakes of coaches and wagons can be run in the space available. Meanwhile I am building a British N layout based on a section of the Newcastle to Carlisle line at Wylam.

Due to so many exhibition commitments with the business, *Die Lötschbergbahn* has had few outings to date.

Above
SBB Cargo and BLS Cargo join forces on a Hupac 'rolling road' service as a BLS 485 with an intermodal heads in the other direction.

Below
The garden centre is a mecca for families. PTT post buses are a common sight. Some very fit (or mad) cyclists are braving this mountainous area.

On the Bern – Lötschberg – Simplon

Ausserberg

In the Valais region **Peter Marriott** found an attractive station to model.
Photographs by the author.

Modellers are keen to find small stations in attractive locations with a small yard that combines scenic appeal and railway interest. Ausserberg on the south ramp of the BLS Lötschberg mountain line is one such station.

The village of Ausserberg lies in the Canton of Valais at an altitude of 1,008m above sea level on the northern slope of the Rhône valley, and consists of a number of scattered settlements with a population of 650.

The station is located on the south ramp of the Lötschberg mountain line at 931m a.s.l., not far from the centre of Trogdorf, which is the main part of Ausserberg. In addition to the railway, local transport is supplied by a Post bus service linking the station with Trogdorf village and Visp on the Rhône valley main line.

Ausserberg is a typical Valais mountain village with a well-preserved centre in a diverse landscape which has its own microclimate. Natural irrigation and fertile soil makes fruit farming (cherries, plums, apples) and arable farming (potatoes, grains) possible up to 1,580m a.s.l.

Lötschberg South Ramp

The Lötschberg line is the main BLS artery, linking Spiez (on Lake Thun) with Brig, near the entrance of the Simplon tunnel to Italy. Construction of the 14.6km Lötschberg tunnel commenced in 1906 and was completed in 1913. The route from Spiez to Brig was converted to double track between 1976 and 1992.

There are regular, generally hourly, local rail services on the south ramp as well as the regional expresses to Spiez and Bern. Some of these now run through to Domodossola in Italy. Since the opening of the new base tunnel, the number of freights over the classic Lötschberg route has dramatically diminished, and of course the InterCity and EuroCity trains no longer use this route unless the base tunnel is closed.

Left
Looking north across the small yard near the tunnel portal in July 2015. By this time it was unusual to see a loco-hauled train because most passenger services were using the AlpTransit base tunnel.

Below
The station building in June 2012.

Above
Looking towards Bern along the station platforms.

Left
Former transformer tower and wooden shed looking across the valley.

Top right
Two BLS Traxx locos head an intermodal train north.

Right
Two Lötschberger class 535 units about to leave the platform towards Bern.

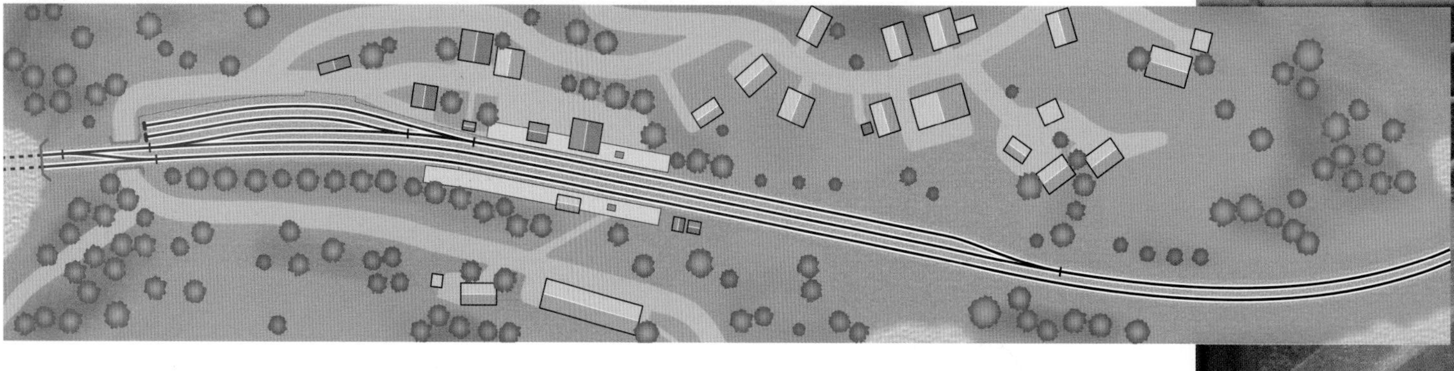

I sat by the line for three hours in June 2018 and witnessed three light engine movements and six freights in addition to the hourly passenger services in each direction. One of the passenger services was a NINA unit substituting for a class 535 Lötschberger unit.

There is a classic walk along the Lötschberg southern approach from Hohtenn via Ausserberg, Eggerberg, and Lalden to Brig. Ausserberg station is an intermediate point on the Lötschberg South Ramp walking trail, which parallels the south ramp of the railway as it descends the northern flank of the Rhône valley into Brig. The 23km walk offers views south over the valley. Walking time from Hohtenn to Ausserberg is 3 hours, from Ausserberg to Eggerberg 1 hour 45 minutes, and Eggerberg to Lalden 50 minutes. BLS produce useful leaflets with maps for walkers. The walks may be modified by using local BLS rail services to cover parts of the route.

Ausserberg station

The station is situated on a shelf on the mountainside overlooking the Rhône valley, with three running lines through the station and three platforms linked by an underpass. At the north end of the station is a small yard of two sidings which is now used by permanent way vehicles. The main running lines are signalled for bi-directional running.

There is a main station building, which has recently been renovated, on one platform, plus a waiting shelter on the other. Near the main station building is a wooden goods shed. Several years ago there were several modern BLS Portakabin structures adjacent to the track but these have been replaced by a permanent shed. Just behind the main station building is a hotel and several car parking spaces.

Modelling Ausserberg station

Creating the look of a BLS station in model form is more than just running BLS locomotives and rolling stock on the layout. There are many detailing products available to make a good model representation.

Models of BLS station buildings are available from a number of companies, including Faller and Kibri.

Fides Press (**www.hobby-shop.ch**) and Tip Top Modell (**www.tiptopmodell.ch**) offer laser-cut kits for station buildings – the Tip Top Modell range actually includes a kit for Ausserberg.

The BLS changed its corporate livery around 2006 and today the main colours are silver, bright green, and dark blue. Their posters, timetables, ticket machines, station nameboards and other station paraphernalia all contain elements of these colours. BLS modified its signage again in early 2017. Authentic posters and signs can be custom made by taking photographs of the posters you want to reproduce then reducing them on a computer and printing them in colour on the best quality paper.

Above
Station building and goods shed, 25th June 2018.

Above left
Ticket machine, vending machine, and arrivals indicator under the station canopy.

Left
The shelter on the platform opposite the station. Note the sign forbidding crossing the tracks.

Collecting leaflets and pocket timetables is also useful for station posters which can be cut out (use a sharp craft knife, a steel ruler, and a cutting board) and sticking onto thin cardboard for miniature posters – I used a glue stick. BLS posters are also available in HO from **www.aubertrain.com**

Prototypical catenary for the BLS network is available in HO from Sommerfeldt (**www.sommerfeldt.de**) and Barin Modell (**www.barinmodell.com**).

BLS locomotives and rolling stock are readily available in N and HO; the selection is more limited in TT and O.

Rietze (**www.rietze.de**) produce a number of station accessories, such as bus stops, Selecta vending machines, and Automat ticket machines, though the SBB ticket machine would need to be repainted in BLS silver and green.

Ticket validation machines, Selecta vending machines, PTT post boxes, footpath and post bus signs, waste bins, station seats, BLS tunnel portals, and more accessories are available from Modellbau Atelier (**www.mbapiro.ch**).

Microscale (**www.microscale.ch**) makes a good range of detailing accessories including advertising boards, illuminated station signs, and 'Do Not Cross The Line' notices. In addition they produce signals and other accessories including the modern station information centre and shelter.

Above right
Station building, 25th June 2018.

Below
Almost a track plan, looking towards Brig.

Another company with a growing range of station accessories suitable for standard and narrow gauge Swiss lines is Albula Modell, whose range includes platform signs, seats, vending machines, salt bins, rubbish bins, newspaper distribution racks, and lots more. (**www.albulamodell.ch**)

Rietze also make a large range of model coaches and buses suitable for Swiss layouts including the Post buses that are seen at many BLS stations, plus BLS buses as seen in the Emmental area. Other buses and coaches are available from Busch (**www.busch-model.info**), EYRO (**www.eyro.ch**), Schuco (**www.schuco.de**), and also VK Modelle (**www.vk-modelle.de**), amongst others.

Modern Swisscom telephone boxes are still a common sight at BLS stations. Brawa produces a model which is illuminated and nicely modelled with clear plastic windows and interior detail.

Left
Two BLS Lötschberger class 535 units have just left the platform (out of view to the left) heading towards Bern.

Below left
The steep slope and chalets behind the station.

Above
Diesel tractor Tm 98 85 5235 091-6 CH BLS on 26th June 2012.

Below
Two BLS Lötschberger class 535 units working from Bern to Brig have just left the north tunnel portal.

bls

186 904
D-XR

Left
A BLS Lötschberger class 535 unit arriving en route from Domodossola to Bern on 26th June 2018.

Right
Looking towards Eggerberg and Brig with a class 535 unit in the platform.

Below left
Two Crossrail 186s (904 leading) heading towards Spiez with a train of LKW Walter trailers. Note the gradient dropping away immediately beyond the station area. Details like the transformer on the catenary mast would be important for a model.

Below
Hotel Bahnhof to the left, new shed in the centre, and station to the right.

For more information

The Modellbauteam Köln made a splendid model of Ausserberg station several years ago. It is featured at:

www.modellbahn-links.de/modellbahn/modellbahn-anlagen/modellbauteam-koeln-bls-nord-u-suedrampe/

Since March 2013 the layout has been permanently located in the Good Night Inn hotel in Brig but it is not yet open for regular viewing.

www.bls.ch/en has rail timetables plus information about events and excursions on the BLS network (in English).

The European Rail Map (**www.europeanrailtimetable.eu**) is a good way to see BLS routes in their European setting.

The *Eisenbahn Journal* Special *Die BLS – Eine moderne Alpenbahn* contains some superb photographs. It was followed by the *Lötschbergbahn* Special in 2013.

DVDs are available from companies such as Ticket to Ride, MITV, Perren, and Lineside Videos.

The Swiss Railways motive power handbook from Platform 5 was updated in 2016.

The Swiss Railways Society produces a full colour quarterly magazine and has published a useful range of books.

www.SwissRailSoc.org.uk

Information about travel and accommodation in Switzerland can be found at **www.myswitzerland.com**

For general information on walking in Switzerland, see **http://wanderland.myswitzerland.com/en/welcome.cfm** and **www.wandern.ch**

BLS have published a book of walks based on their Lötschberger services.

http://www.loetschberger.ch/wanderbuch?utm_source=enews_wettbewerb&utm_medium=nl&utm_campaign=wanderbuch

Right
The line between Eggerberg and Ausserberg a minute or so before the train arrives at Ausserberg.

Below
Typical local chalets.

Behind the scenes on the metre gauge

MOB service stock

Michael Farr believes the Montreux Oberland Bernois *wagons de service* have the 'X factor'. *Prototype photographs by the author. Scale drawings courtesy BVA/La Raillère.*

Even in these days of rail standardisation, you can still find a variety of rolling stock of all ages amongst the *wagons de service*. On my favourite Swiss railway, the MOB, these range from ancient vans now used for storage (*magasin* wagons) to special vehicles either built on old chassis or completely new wagons constructed to carry modern aids to track maintenance such as bulldozers and excavators. To fit them into the metre gauge loading gauge is quite a challenge.

Having been lucky enough to acquire a copy of the official list of wagons in active stock, I found that the numbering is somewhat random. While the service stock has the prefix X, ballast wagons and some bogie flats are actually listed among the *wagons merchandises* – normal freight stock. For this feature I am concentrating on the X series.

In addition to the vehicles in the MOB list, I found withdrawn wagons tucked away in sidings, notably outside the works at Chernex and at Fontanivent on the spur which used to form the Clarens-Chailly-Blonay tram route. Although many station yards are now totally bereft of goods vehicles due to the lack of goods traffic, Zweisimmen yard has been worth exploring, as well as the sidings at St.Stephan and both at the airstrip at Oey and in nearby Saanen station. The withdrawn wagons usually carry a white paper sticker with HORS SERVICE printed in red.

Over the years there have been many wagons allocated to *le service de la voie* and fleet numbers have generally been duplicated. The appended table includes most of those recently listed and those for which HOm models are known to have been produced.

For details of the older vehicles, readers are referred to the books edited by Jean-Louis Rochaix for BVA/La Raillère (ISBN 2-88 125-008-4 and ISBN 2-88 125-009-2; la.raillere@bluewin.ch) and the massive tome, appropriately titled *Le Grand Livre du MOB*, by authors including Patrick Belloncle and published by Viafer/Cabri (ISBN 3-95222494-2-4; viafer@cabri.ch).

Whilst Bemo for some years included models of Rhätische Bahn service stock in their range, they took longer to issue their first model of a genuine MOB X series van: they finished the standard brown van with the number X 7. In September 2010 it was at St.Stephan on the Lenk branch. MOB brown vans are painted in several different shades of this colour (as well as subtleties caused by weathering) but photographs make it clear that the shade of brown used by Bemo is extremely accurate.

If you want to run a rake of service vehicles on your layout you can build them yourself from scratch or, in some cases, adapt commercial models such as those by Bemo.

Alternatively two small specialist model firms, Friho at Lenk (friholenk@bluewin.ch) and Buly at Aigle (buly@ch), offer ready-to-run examples of several MOB *wagons de service*. These are usually produced in limited runs and sold on a first-come, first-served basis; due to the large amount of handwork required they are not cheap. Not surprisingly, those which are constructed from etched and cast metal parts are more expensive than those adapted from Bemo items.

In addition to the service vehicles described here, many rebuilt from former MOB goods rolling stock, the railway has recently invested heavily in new motive power and specialised vehicles; wagons have also been bought from the Rhätische Bahn and the Zentralbahn. Friho already lists models of some of these.

Below
The Malutram model of MOB Gm4/4 diesel No.2003 heads a ballast train with wagons Kkm-u 711, X 49, X 50, and Fd-k 901 and 902.

Right
Two overhead line maintenance vans, numbered OX1 and 2, were built in 1907-8 by Ringhoffer. 2 was demolished after a derailment in 1983 but 1, now classified X 1 and nicknamed *Le Caquelon*, survived and has usually been stabled at Château D'Oex. OX1 originally carried a livery of 'Bordeaux' red; in September 2007 X 1 was painted orange with a white horizontal stripe. Friho plan to offer a model in 2018/9.

Drawings reproduced to 1:87 for HOm.

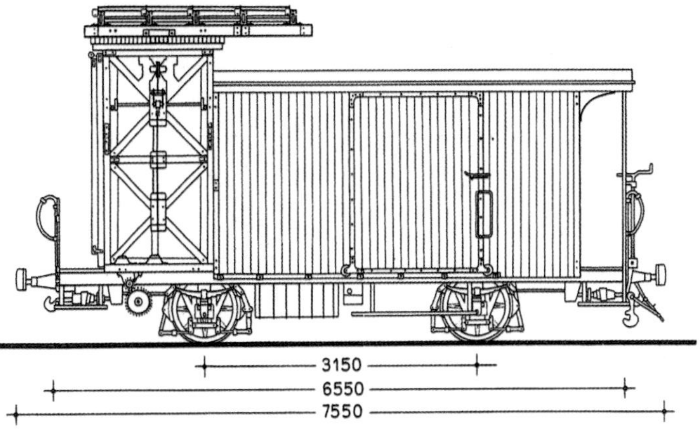

Below left and below
The second replacement X 2 was a conversion of Gk 505 which formerly carried the green 'Sprite' advertising livery. The vinyl lettering was peeled away but the wording was still visible due to the surrounding green paint having faded. It was photographed at Chernex in May 2008; in July 2009 it was stabled at Fontanivent. Both Buly and Friho have offered models of the latest X 2 van.

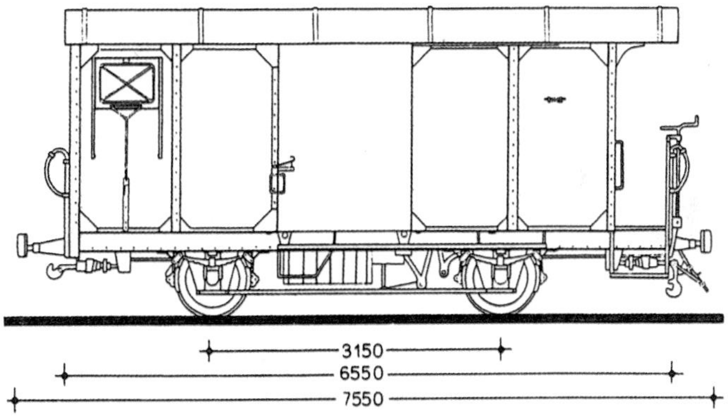

Below
Buly has converted the Bemo model of Gk 505 by mounting on the roof a neat platform with demountable guard rails and cutting away part of the roof to provide access from the platform. The body has been lightly sprayed so the original advertising elements are still faintly visible.

Below and below right
The Friho model has more detail with spotlight, access ladder, and hooks to hold the coil of cabling under the light. The roof-mounted platform has a patterned silver floor with eight individual supports and the guard rails hinge upwards. The body is finished smoothly in green although none of the former 'Sprite' wording is visible. This model is naturally more expensive than the Buly one due to the additional detailing.

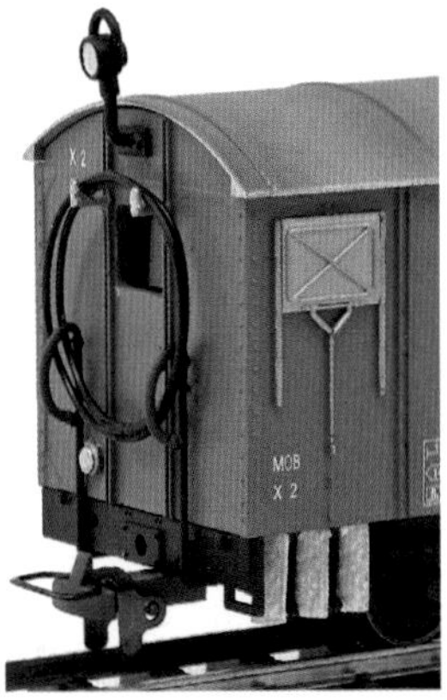

Above

A new overhead line van with roof platform roof was created in 1996 by converting van Gk 519, re-using the number X 2. This was replaced in 2002 and the van later became X 4. The platform mounting points can still be seen.

Above

Van Gk 555, which has smooth sides instead of the more common planks, was cascaded to service stock in 1980 and renumbered X 3. By 2002 the vehicle (with paint peeling) bore the *Hors Service* stickers (now all too familiar on MOB freight stock); it was withdrawn in 2015. Seen, looking the worse for wear, among mainly withdrawn stock, at Fontanivent in July 2009.

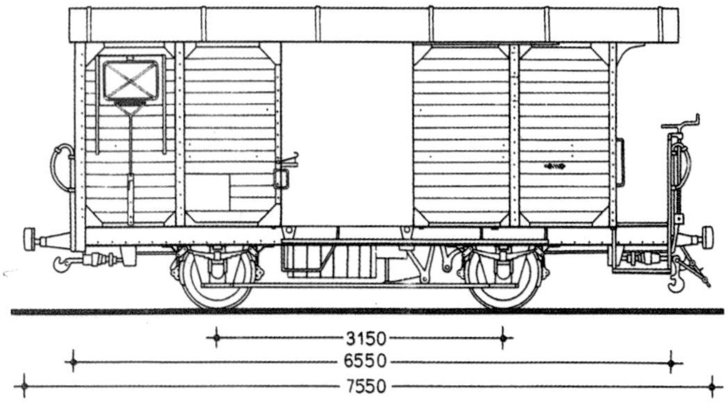

Right and top right

X 6 began life as Gk 552 but was transferred to service stock in 1985; in July 2009 it stood *Hors Service* at Fontanivent; it was withdrawn in 2015. Friho offered a model in their 2000 list.

Left and right

Bemo chose X 7 for their first MOB service stock van, delivering the models in September 2009. Although listed as active stock, I could not find it when visiting the railway in July 2009, but it was on a siding at St.Stephan in September 2010.

Above

Four of the brown vans which were transferred to service stock. X 7 (the first MOB X series vehicle from Bemo) with X 3, X 6, and X 61, which have all been produced by Friho.

Above
Four-wheeled wagon X 8 carried a stepladder for overhead line maintenance and was usually stabled in the rearmost road of the sidings at Château D'Oex, where it was photographed in September 2010. It was rebuilt in 1987 using the chassis from 1904-vintage wagon Ek 613. It was withdrawn in 2015.

Right
The Friho model of the stepladder trolley off the carrying wagon.

Below
Snowplough X 9 was constructed by fitting a plough to open wagon Lo153 and allocated to Zweisimmen in the 1960s, carrying the name *Snow Bird*; it was renumbered in the X series in 1979.

I was too late to photograph the prototype as a snowplough but fortunately one Sunday in the spring of 2007 a supporter of the Blonay-Chamby line noticed the vehicle at Chernex without the plough. This could indicate only one thing – demolition! As it represented one of the first batches of short wagons, built by SIG in 1903, the BC decided it was worth saving and after some frantic telephone calls on the Monday the deal was done.

These wagons were, unusually for Switzerland, mounted on bogies due to the exceedingly sharp curves on the MOB when built though these have since been eased.

The refurbished vehicle was presented to the public on the BC at Whitsun 2009, with its original number (Lo153) restored.

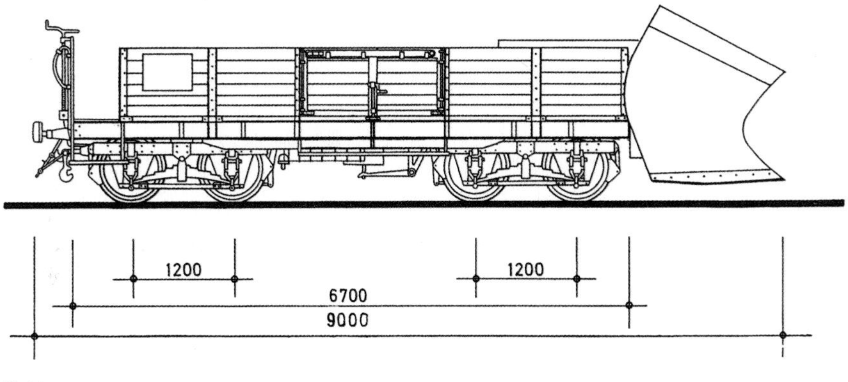

Below
Snowplough X 9, created by fitting a red snowplough to one of the original short bogie open wagons, is offered by Friho as a hand-built model.

Right
The number 11 has always been carried by a snowplough and the actual plough (at times carrying the name *L'Étoile des Neiges*) has been passed from one to another. The third number 11 is one of three generally similar snowploughs built to a design of the Chemins de fer du Jura, using lengths of rail to provide the extra weight required. No.11 was spotted at Zweisimmen in July 2009.

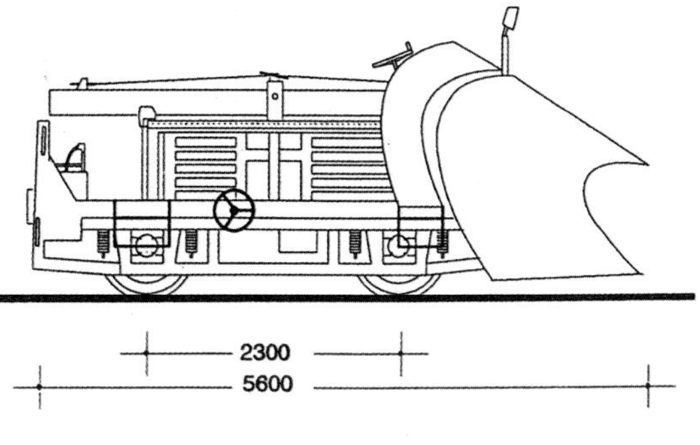

Above
X 13 was a four-wheel flat used for transporting bogies, formerly Ek 607, transferred to service stock in 1973 and scrapped in 1990. Friho produced a model, supplied carrying Glion-Naye wagon Z 16.

Right
X 14 began life in 1905 as Ek 620 and was renumbered into service stock in 1976 when fitted with a small Atlas crane. This was removed in 1999 since when X 14 has been used to carry a rubbish skip. In September 2010 it was seen in a line of X-series vehicles at Zweisimmen.

Above
Built in 1914 as Rko 825, X 15 was transferred to service stock in 1976/7. Despite being suitable for long (14.5m) loads, it is listed as a flat wagon for ballast, although when seen parked at Fontanivent in September 2007 (*above right*) it was being used for track components. The model (*right*) is by Friho.

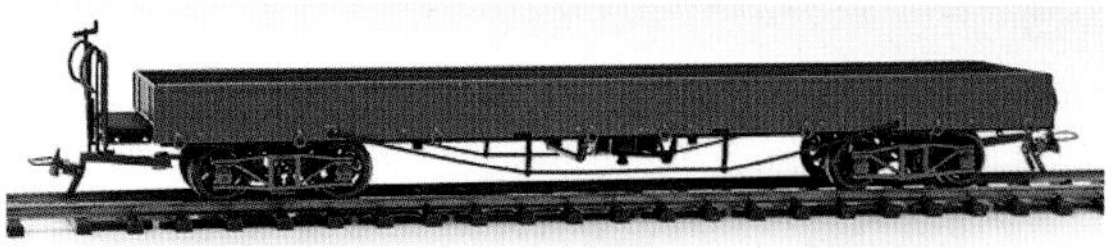

Left and right
Four-wheeled tank wagon X 16 began life in 1902 on the adjoining CEV (Chemins de fer électriques veveysans). It was taken into MOB stock in 1978. Photographed at Chernex works in September 2007 carrying *Hors Service* labels. It was withdrawn in 2014. The model is by Friho.

Left and right
Open wagon Ek 653, built by SIG in 1905, was converted in 1980 to tanker X 17 to hold diesel fuel. It received a larger tank (from a lorry) seven years later and by May 2008 was stored at Zweisimmen *Hors Service*. It was withdrawn in 2009. Friho produced models with the first small (*above right*) and the later larger tank.

Left
X 18 was another van (formerly Gk 551) taken into service stock since the demise of commercial goods traffic. It is branded *Transport Compresseur* and was based at Montbovon, though in July 2009 (when still listed as active stock) it was at Fontanivent. It was withdrawn in 2015.

Above
Low steel side open wagon X 19 was originally Kk 752. MOB describe its use as *transports fraiseurs*, for carrying milling equipment. It was stabled at Chernex station in July 2009. It was withdrawn in 2014. Friho listed a model in 2004.

Left
The chassis of X 20 was originally under Uace-k 882. It has undergone two transformations. In 1984 its first use it was to transport bogies for the 6000 series locos between maintenance depots at Zweisimmen and Montreux, and Chernex works. In 2002 it was adapted to carry the excavator nicknamed *Muck* but in July 2009 it was stabled at Saanen carrying two skips. It was withdrawn in 2014.

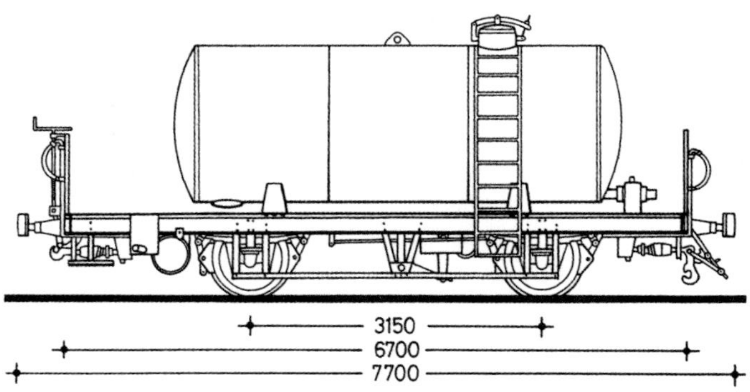

X 16

Above and below
X 21 had the distinction of being the oldest extant van on the MOB, having been built by SIG in 1901. It was earmarked for *transport de bourreuses* (tampers), becoming X 101 in 1965 and X 21 fourteen years later. In both 2007 and 2009 it was to be seen in Chernex works yard. Due to its historic significance it was passed to the Blonay-Chamby in 2013.

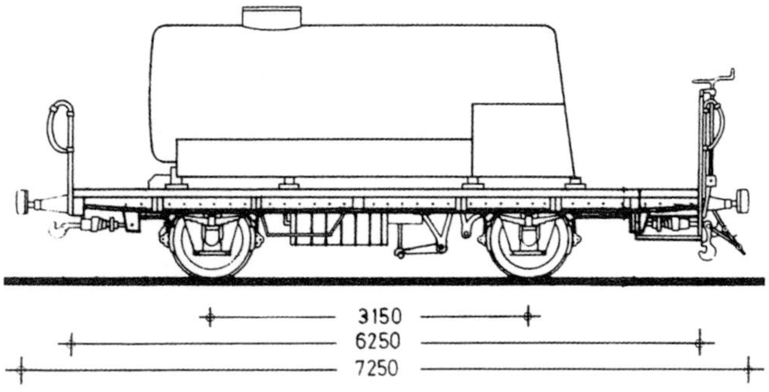

X 17

Above
1905-vintage van X 22 (originally Gk 517) transferred to service stock in 1989 as a storage (*magasin*) wagon. It was photographed at Zweisimmen in July 2009. It was withdrawn in 2016. A model was listed by Friho in 2000.

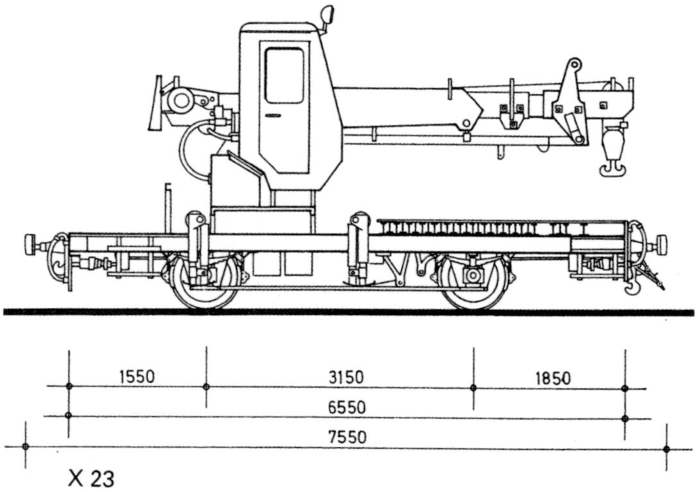

X 23

Left and right
Since an Austin Western crane was mounted on the chassis of Ek 614 in 1989, the resultant X 23 has proved a reliable workhorse. Seen at Zweisimmen in September 2010.

Below
The Friho model of X 24, rebuilt from lowside Rkmo 817 as a mess coach in 1988 and destroyed in an explosion the same year.

Right
The Buly model of X 23.

Below left and right
X 25 is mounted on a pair of the original standard gauge transporter bogies which had formerly been used on cement silo wagon Uace-k 883. It was rebuilt as a low-floor bogie wagon designed with substantial ramps for roll on/roll-off loading of road vehicles. The photograph of the empty vehicle taken at Chernex in September 2007 shows that all the pipes and tanks are exposed so they would present quite a challenge to model in detail.
X 25 was spotted again at both Schonried and Zweisimmen in July 2009 carrying an excavator.

Left
Four-wheeled tank wagon X 29 began life in 1971 as Uh-k 897. With a capacity of 17,000 litres and fitted with a pump, it was photographed at Lenk in September 2007. Two years later it was stabled at St.Stephan ready to be used for cleaning gutters! It was on the Friho future models list in 2009.

Right
X32 was allocated in 1999 to carrying skips for glass for recycling. It was not seen on the line in July 2009 and the skips were on X 20. It was withdrawn in 2014.

Left and right
La Bobinette **carries cable drums, having been converted from Ek 616 in 1991. Like X 8, the vehicle was usually tucked away in the back siding at Château D'Oex where it was photographed in September 2010. Friho offered a hand-built (metal) model (*below*).**

Left
X 36 – 39 are carrier bogies placed in service in 1990 for transporting 800mm gauge MTGN vehicles to the workshops. Seen at Montreux in September 2010.

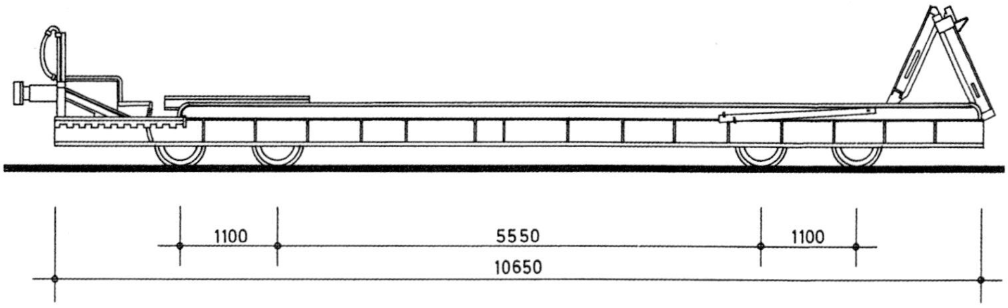

X 25

Left and right
Heavy duty crane wagon X 40 can lift loads of up to 5.8 tonnes with its Palfinger crane powered by a Deutz diesel engine; four outriggers are provided for stability. In July 2009 the crane truck was seen coupled to Gm4/4 diesel locomotive No.2003.

Below and right
The Buly model, issued in 2010, includes two sets of outriggers (of different lengths) which can be slid into holes on the wagon. The very detailed crane pivots and is hinged in three sections with simulated hydraulics. Two extra jibs are provided, offering a longer reach when used as a static model. The low body (complete with a patterned footplate on top) is mounted on a Bemo chassis.

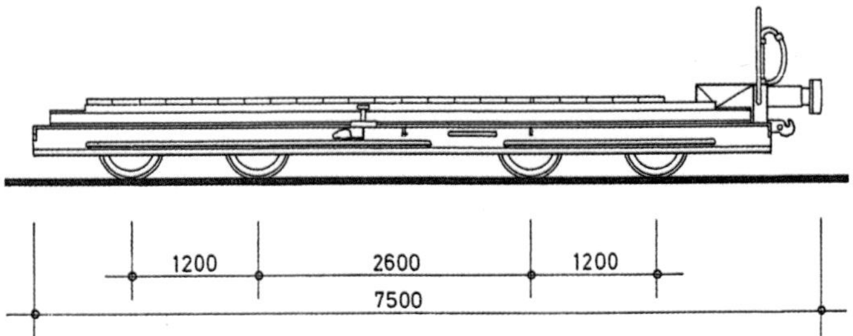

X 41

Above and right
X 41 was built in 1986 using an original *truck transporteur* (Ua 851) for standard gauge wagons. Here at Montbovon in September 2010 it carries a road mounted access platform. It was withdrawn in 2013.

Right and below
X 45 was lurking at the end of a siding at Fontanivent hiding its load of a high-level crane trolley under a blue tarpaulin in July 2009. While most other vehicles in the rake were *Hors Service*, X 45 (named *La Colinette*) was ready for use. This siding was once the main line of the Clarens-Chailly-Blonay Tramway; the adjoining track served the line's carriage shed.

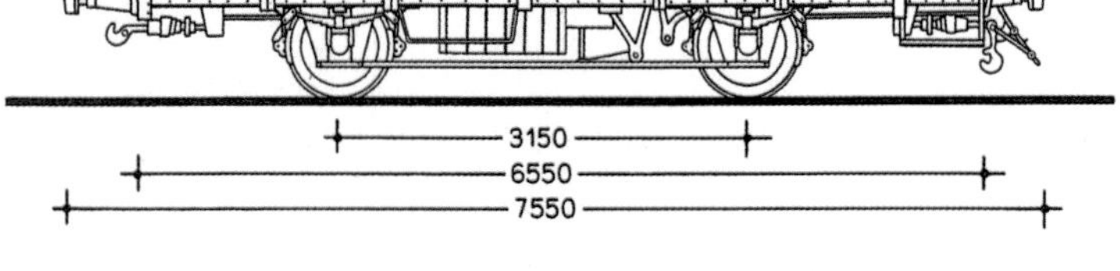

Above, above right, and left

Three Rko bogie flat wagons were transferred to service stock in 1993 as X 46, 47, and 48. They have end walls and pivoted stanchions and are used to carry long loads such as pipes, or sleepers. Seen at Château D'Oex in July 2009.

Right

In September 2010, X 48 was stabled in a siding at Chernex station carrying bogies under sheets.

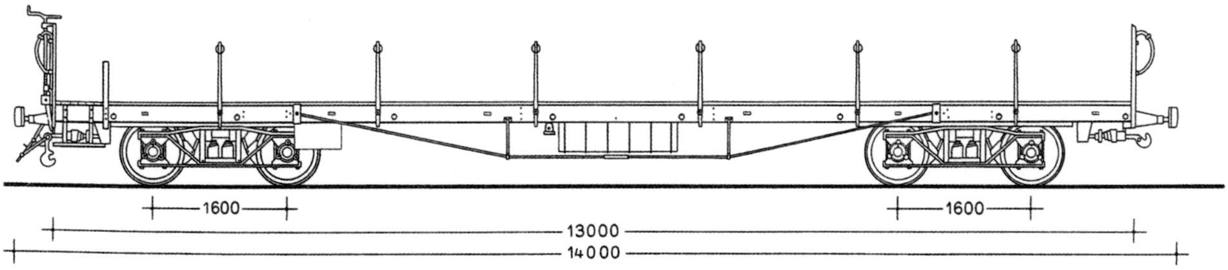

Right and below

From time to time the MOB has borrowed wagons from the RhB, though these have different couplings.
X 49 and 50 were adapted as converters, 49 having RhB couplings at the Zweisimmen end and 50 towards Montreux. They are fitted with ballast weights for stability.
In May 2009 X 50 was found at Château D'Oex station.
In September 2010 both wagons were at Montbovon with some of the Talbot ballast wagons acquired from the Rhätische Bahn.

Far right

Buly has produced models of X49 and 50, the converter wagons for coupling to Rhätische Bahn rolling stock, carrying skips of ballast.

MOB service stock X-series vehicles

No.	status	description	to service stock	original no.	model
X 1	extant	overhead line van	1907	OX1	Friho (planned for 2018/9)
X 2^{II}	see X 4	overhead line van	renumbered 1986	Gk 552	Friho
X 2^{III}	extant	overhead line van	rebuilt 3/2001	Gk 505	Buly and Friho (ex 'Sprite')
X 3	w. 2015	van	renumbered 1980	Gk 553	Friho
X 4	w. 2015	van (ex overhead line)	renumbered 2002	X 2^{I}	
X 6	w. 2015	van	renumbered 1985	Gk 519	Friho
X 7	extant	van	renumbered 1985	Gk 557	Friho, Bemo
X 8	w. 2015	overhead ladder wagon *La Zibeline,*	converted 1987	Gk 513	
X 9	to B-C 2007	snowplough	renumbered, plough fitted 1979	Lo 153	Friho restored as open wagon 200
			plough transferred to X 60		
X 10	extant	snowplough	1968/1986		
X 11^{III}	extant	snowplough (weighted with rails)	1964		
X 12	extant	snowplough	1964		
X 13	scrapped	flat for bogies	1973, scrapped 1990	Ek 607	Friho (supplied with Glion-Naye wagon Z
X 14	sold* 2015	flat for a rubbish skip	1976	Ek 620	formerly with a small crane, removed 199
X 15	extant	bogie open with sides (for ballast)	rebuilt 1976, renumbered 1977	Rko 825	
X 16	w. 2014	diesel tank	to MOB 1977, renumbered 1978	CEV Oc 40	
X 17^{II}	w. 2009	diesel tank	rebuilt 1980, 1982, 1987	Ek 653, X 17^{I}	Friho
X 18	w. 2015	van	renumbered 1980	Gk 551	
X 19	w. 2014	bogie flat with low (metal) sides	renumbered 1980	Kkm or Kki 752	Friho
X 20	w. 2013	flat wagon	rebuilt 1984	Uace-k 882^{III}	
		to carry spare bogies of 6000 series locos between Chernex Works and Zweisimmen depot, now used for *Muck* excavator			
X 21	to B-C 2013	bogie van	renumbered 1985	K 101, X 101	
X 22	w. 2016	van	renumbered 1989	Gk 517	Friho
X 23	extant	flat with Austin Western crane	rebuilt/renumbered 1989	Ek 614	Buly
X 24	scrapped	mess coach	built 1988, destroyed 1988	Rkmo 817	Friho
X 25	extant	bogie flat with end loading,	rebuilt and renumbered 1989	X 4	
X 29^{II}	extant	tank (for water)	rebuilt/renumbered 1990	OC 81^{II}/Uah-k 81^{II} /Uh-k 897	Friho
		with pump for clearing gutters			
X 30	scrapped	pair of rail bolsters	scrapped 2001	X 80+81, then 80	Friho
X 32^{I}	w. 2014	rail barrier wagon; then for skips	renumbered 1985, rebuilt 1998	Kk 751 / X 82 (1979)	
X 32^{II}	extant	bogie van	converted 12/2015	BD32 postal van	Friho (planned for 2018/9)
X 35	extant	cable drum wagon *La Bobinette*	rebuilt/renumbered 1991	Ek 616	Friho
X 36-39	extant	bogies for transporting 800mm gauge MTGN cars	1990		
X 40	extant	(Palfinger hydraulic crane wagon	rebuilt/renumbered 1996	Gk 528	
X 41	extant 2007	flat wagon for crane on road wheels	rebuilt 1895/1986	Ua 851	
X 42	w. 2006	bogie flat	renumbered 1986	Ua 852	
X 43	scrapped	stores van for electrical dept.	acquired 1992, scrapped 1998	GFM D 421	
X 44	sold 2005	stores van for electrical dept.	acquired 1988	GFM D 422	Buly to CF Baie de Somme
X 45	extant	ladder wagon (c/f X 8) *La Colinette*	rebuilt 1996	Ek 611	
X 46	extant	bogie flat with stanchions	renumbered 1993	Rko 822	
X 47	extant	bogie flat with stanchions	renumbered 1993	Rko 823	
X 48	extant	bogie flat with stanchions	renumbered 1993	Rko 828	
X 49	extant	MOB/RhB barrier wagon	renumbered 1996	Uh-k 890	Buly (as a pair)
X 50	extant	MOB/RhB barrier wagon	renumbered 1996	Uh-k 899	Friho (in preparation)
X 52	w. 2013	bogie flat for electrical dept.	acquired 1998	GFM Rkm 912	
X 53	extant	flat for rolling container, rail	rebuilt/renumbered 2000	Uh-k 891	Friho
X 54	extant	flat for rolling container, rail	rebuilt/renumbered 2000	Uh-k 892	Friho
X 55	extant	flat for rolling container, rail	rebuilt/renumbered 2000	Uh-k 894	Friho
X 56	extant	flat for rolling container, rail	rebuilt/renumbered 2000	Uh-k 900	Friho
X 57	extant	bogie rail transporter with winches	acquired 2000	GFM O 155/OM 925/Uah-k 1107	
X 59	extant	van	renumbered 2006	Gk 507 (Ausoni)	Friho
X 60	extant	snowplough (plough from X 9)	renumbered 2006	Uce-k 889	Friho
X 61	w. 2014	van (storage)			Friho
X 62/3/4	extant	rail transport wagons (triple set)	converted 2007	originally for CEV	
X 65	extant	van	renumbered 2014	Gk 502 (AWZ)	
X 70	extant	flat for Montreux glass skip	converted 2013	Uce-k 885; skip from X 32^{I}	
X 303	preserved	rail grinder	acquired 1965	to BC 1992, restored as original Bienne Tramways water vehicle	
X 402	extant	service van (bogies from GFM Uah-k 1106)	rebuilt 2001	Hack-v 402 (1973)	Friho
	w. = withdrawn		* to The Netherlands	*For more detail of all vehicles, see* www.x-rail.ch	

Above and above right
The MOB acquired two flat bogie wagons from the Gruyère – Fribourg – Morat (GFM), Rkmo 906 and 912, in 1996/8 for use in transporting overhead line poles and other equipment for the electrical department. Although X 51 is no longer listed as in active stock, in July 2009 it was on the *Hors Service* line at Fontanivent (*above*); X 52 (which is still listed) was a little way along the line at Chernex (*above right*). It was withdrawn in 2013.

Below
X 53, X 54, X 56 are former flat wagons rebuilt in 2000 and renumbered. The Friho models carry various loads.

Left and right
'Ausoni' advertising van Gk 507 was renumbered into service stock as X 59 by simply painting over the old number. In 2008 it stood at the end of a siding at Zweisimmen; the following year it was stabled at St.Stephan on the Lenk branch, keeping company with various other goods wagons.

Left
Friho did the same change on the Bemo model (ref.2274 317).

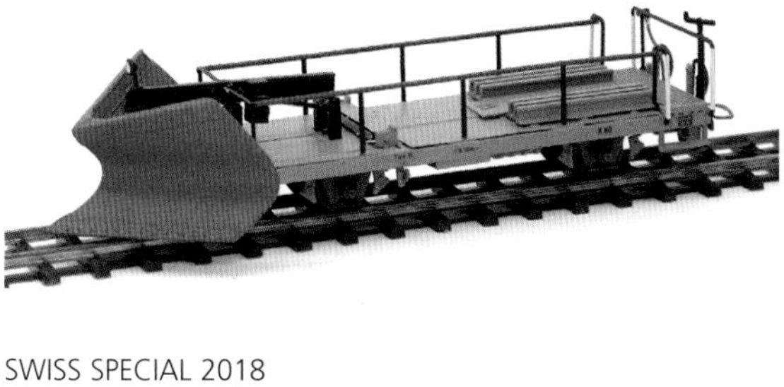

Left
The chassis of cement silo wagon Uce-k 889 built by Vevey as recently as 1992 was renumbered X 60 and fitted with the plough from X 9. Noted at Lenk in 2007 and 2008, it was photographed at Zweisimmen a year later. The model is by Friho.

Above right
This 1905-vintage van was transferred to service stock in 2007 as X 61; it was seen at Zweisimmen in September 2010. Withdrawn in 2014. Friho have produced a model of this vehicle.

Left
Although numbered in MOB service stock, X 62, 63, and 64 were originally used exclusively on the CEV, with extended coupling bars to carry rails. The three-unit rake was put into service on 31st May 2007 and was photographed in the metre gauge yards at Vevey in July 2009. The wagons are actually numbered 61, 62, and 63 even though listed in official records as 62, 63, and 64!

Below
The former AWZ advertising van Gk 502 was transferred to service stock as X 65 in 2014, and like Ausoni van X 59 has only had the number painted over.

Left and above
Bogie van O 819, built by Ringhoffer in 1907, was renumbered briefly J 402 then ran as Hack-v 402 from 1973 to 2001. At that time the works needed a new emergency van and it was extensively rebuilt, emerging with ex-GFM bogies and in the dark blue livery now used for refurbished service stock. For the past five years it has been parked in a siding near Chernex station. Sadly, the Friho hand-built metal model (*below left*) is no longer available.

Left
A pair of bolster wagons for rail transport, modelled by Friho but no longer listed, numbered 80 and 81. Jointly renumbered X 80, by the time they were scrapped in 2001 they were X 30A+B.

Neuburg 1913

Jim Finlayson describes his Swiss metre gauge layout.
Photographs by Rebecca Flynn.

Welcome to Neuburg. The year is 1913 and this intermediate station on the Rhätische Bahn (RhB) is welcoming a VIP family who are using the railway on their journey to the 'Grand Hotel' nearby whose advertisement in Bradshaw's to attract the English states "surrounded by pine forest, with tennis court, own toboggan run and skating rink, along with tea parties". The local traditional band and folk dancers have been called on to provide entertainment whilst their baggage is transferred to the waiting coach for the final leg of their journey. Some crates of beer have been kindly provided by the hotel to refresh the band and dancers.

Below
G2/2+2/2 0-4-4-0T Mallet 22 *Albula* is shunting its mixed train while a G4/5 2-8-0 waits in the loop and a sister loco, fitted with a snow plough, arrives on the station track.

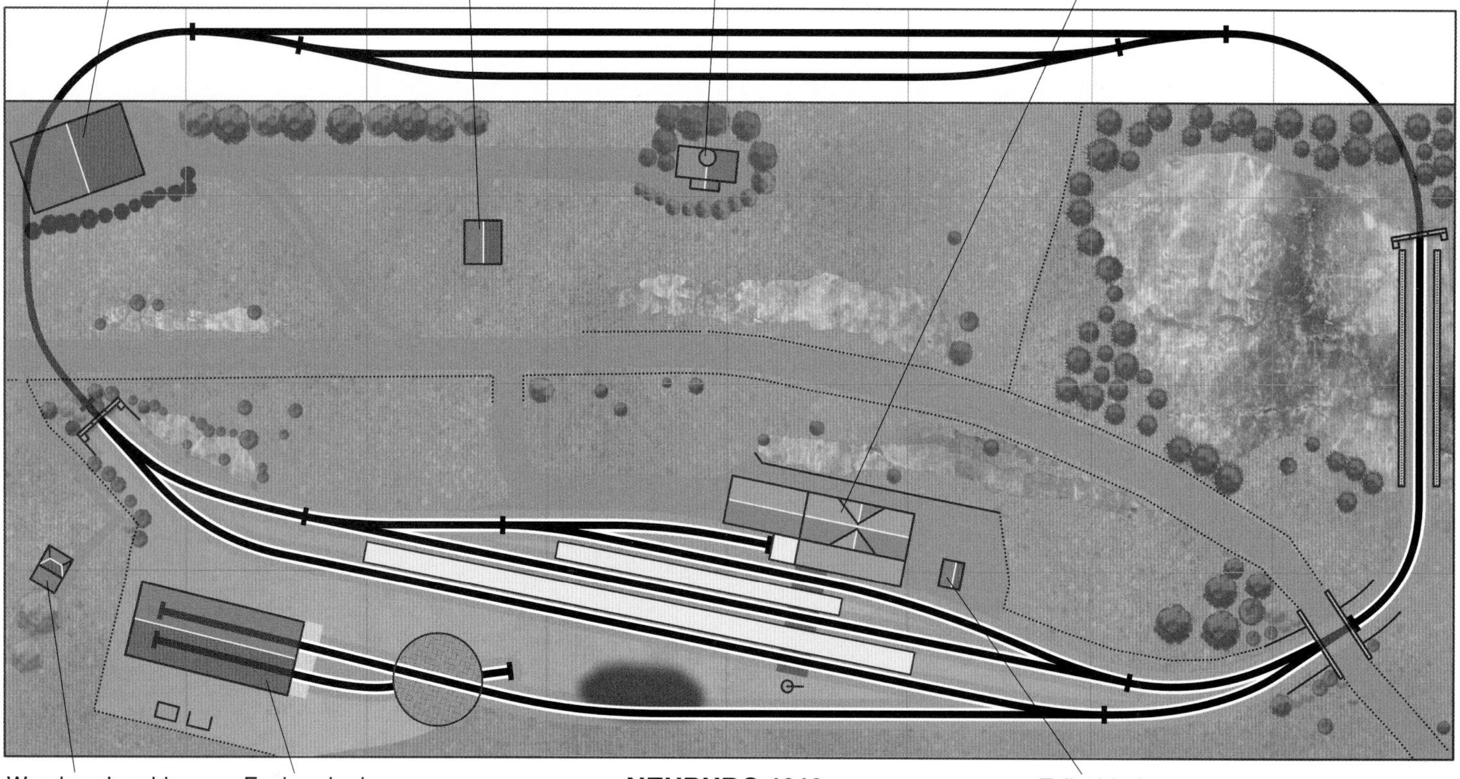

NEUBURG 1913
Overall size: 8' x 4'. Each grid square: 1ft x 1ft.

Below
The hot air balloon flights provide a bird's eye view of the station site. It could almost be a model!

Locals have been pleasantly surprised at the success of the hotel drawing visitors all year round; some thought the idea of winter sports holidays a bit crazy, but they do seem popular! The locals remain unconvinced about the hot air balloon rides the hotel arranges, but if it brings visitors, best not be too critical. The success of winter sports obliged the RhB to introduce a massive snow blower in 1910; it can keep the line open all year round, which has proved to be a lifeline for the surrounding communities.

Talk among the loco and shed crews is to enjoy the good times while they can. Traffic is up and the new G4/5 2-8-0 locomotives were doing well, apart from the tenders on the first batch being too small; they are doing far less damage to the track than the old Mallets. The word from crews who travel much further afield is not so good; the situation in the Balkans is fragile and if things come to the worst, what would we do for coal since every bit is imported? The new-fangled electric locos might find this line hard work, even if they could put up overhead cables with all the tunnels and bridges.

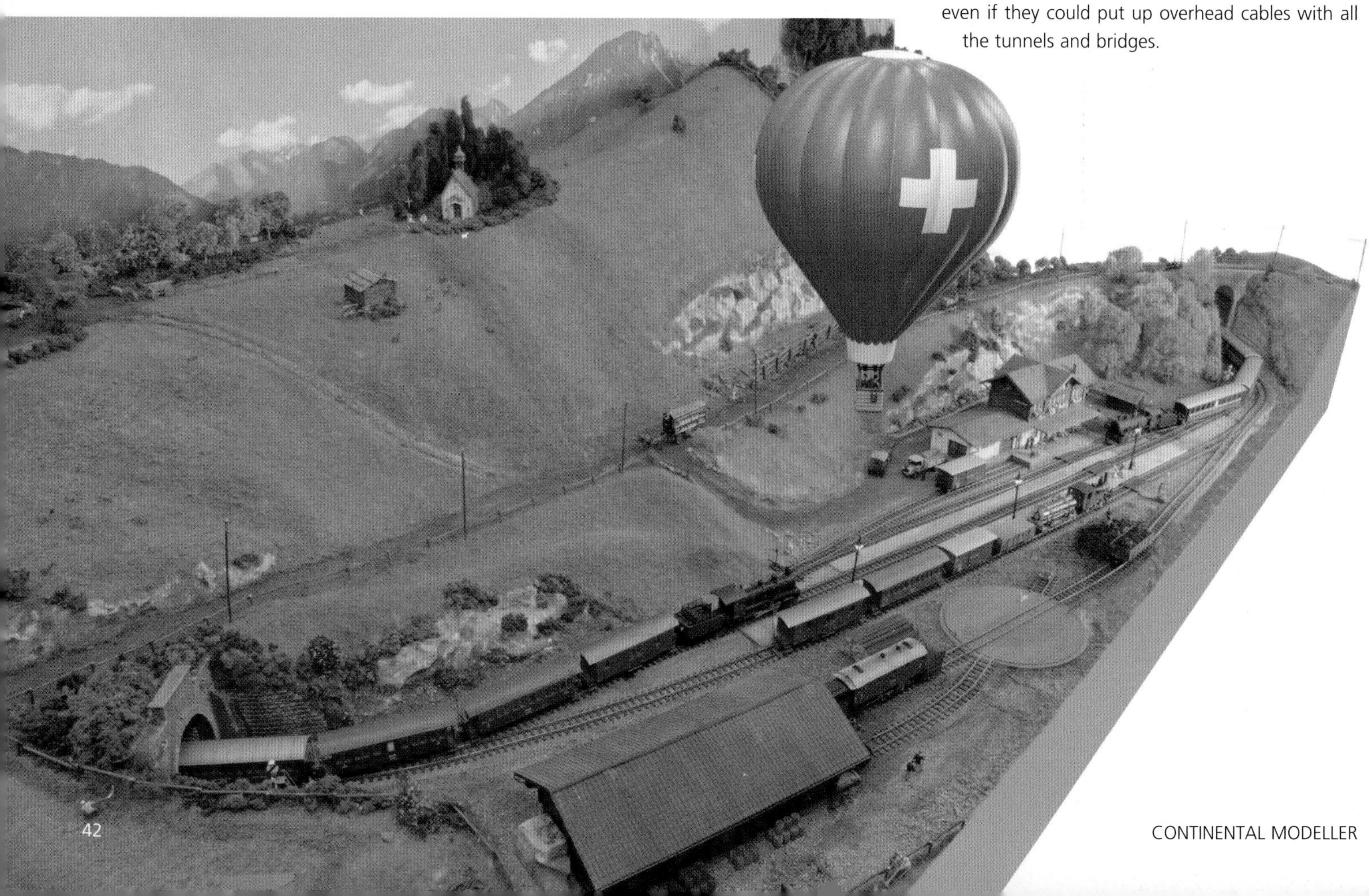

Above
G2/2+2/3 0-4-4-2T Mallet 24 *Chiavenna* being oiled while the new snow blower is brought out for a test run.

Below
G3/4 2-6-0T 1 *Rhätia* pulls in with a mixed local service.

The inspiration

If you are fortunate enough to travel in Switzerland, you cannot help but admire the scenic grandeur and be amazed by the way the railways are constructed: clinging to ledges, spanning chasms, and running through tunnels. In particular, these aspects of the RhB in the Grisons canton captured my attention. This interest was refined after visiting the Albula Museum and understanding some of the social and railway history of the area; I was intrigued by the early steam power used.

Frachtgut
Kiosk
Ankunft
Rh.B. 114
Rh.B.
L 6036

Another piece of the jigsaw which inspired me came from a visit to Miniatur Wunderland in Hamburg – not so much the massive model railway itself but a series of dioramas depicting a section of the Berlin Wall, each showing the same location with the evolving events from the end of the war through the building to the eventual demolition of the wall.

From this evolved the idea of building a layout in a similar vein, depicting the same location in different periods while fulfilling some personal criteria. Specifically, it had to be Swiss, scenic, with a vertical component to the scenery, and it should allow me to either sit back and watch trains run or be more active in operating them. It also had to be compact in design to allow other parts of the larger project to stand beside it.

This layout is the first part of that project and depicts the scene on the line in 1913.

Above
G2/2+2/2 0-4-4-0T Mallet 22 *Albula* collects a wagon from the siding as G4/5 2-8-0 114 waits in the loop to pass 111 with a passenger train.

Although the location is fictional, it seeks to capture the feeling of the Grisons (Graubünden) in the east of Switzerland. The RhB is essentially a single track main line with passing loops either at intermediate stations or indeed wherever the topography allows. The track plan bears more than a passing resemblance to Bergün in 1903 with the loco facilities and turntable to provide interest but with passing loops to allow through traffic.

Baseboards

Baseboard construction is traditional, using a combination of 3" x 1" and 2" x 1" softwood with plywood facings and formers for the scenery. To achieve depth in the scenery there are two frames, base and higher level, with the track being at the higher level. The layout splits into three sections for portability, each board having an open 'crate' to protect the model in transit. The track base is plywood and open plan to allow for scenic detail above and below track level.

The backscene is a single board which is fitted above the fiddle yard at the back of the layout. As the fiddle yard is hidden below the scenery, an LED lighting bar is used to illuminate this area.

Below
Mallet G2/2+2/3 23 *Chiavenna* crossing the stone viaduct over the deep gorge on the approach to Neuburg. Note the hawk circling over the forest.

Left
After crossing the viaduct, the line swings right to pass under the road bridge; the loco is immediately on the first set of points.

Above
G3/4 1 *Rhätia* waits with a mixed local service while a G4/5 comes into the station.

Below
A G3/4 is held on the station track as G4/5 108 overtakes.
Photo: author.

One board has four screw-on height adjustable legs from a well-known Swedish furniture store and is self-supporting. To erect the layout, two trestles support the baseboard while the legs are fitted and adjusted to take account of any floor unevenness. This provides a support for the second and in turn third boards, which have two legs each.

A curtain, a pelmet, and a lighting rig using SMD spotlights complete the public presentation.

Scenery

A significant part of the visual effect of this layout is the height of the scenery, which aims to be representative of the landscape of the region. Construction was by shaping aluminium mesh between plywood formers, covering the mesh with plaster bandage, and finally a coloured plaster skim.

Rock faces are a Heki foil product which is shaped over the mesh and attached with a hot glue gun. It is then blended

into the adjoining area with plaster. Some paint highlighting, real stone, and detailing produces a pleasing result, along with the Noch hard foam viaduct and tunnel mouths.

Trees are made by various techniques: pines by twisted wire with string and texture mounted on lengths of florist's bamboo, painted and textured to give the effect of a trunk. Others are wire armatures bound with florist's tape, and the canopy created with teased felt dressed with foliage.

Meadows are created with static grass blended to give tonal variation and sprinkled with a modicum of bright colour to create the meadow flower effect.

Roads, paths, and the station yard are finely crushed stone.

Reference photographs have been invaluable in determining details such as fencing, rock fall protection, telegraph poles, etc. which do have quite a different look to their British counterparts.

Buildings and ancillaries

The buildings are a mixture of kits and scratchbuilt, based on prototypes. The station and church are Faller kits slightly modified and detailed, while the chalet and engine shed are scratchbuilt. The chalet is based on a typical style using foamboard and stained scribed balsa wood for the walls, plasticard roofing, and 3D-printed windows, shutters, doors, and balconies. Similarly, the engine shed walls are foamboard with stained wooden strips applied, plasticard roof, and 3D-printed windows. The working doors are wooden strips on a brass frame with hinges extended to a mechanism below the baseboard operated by servos. The woodsman's cabins are modified Faller kits and the station toilet block is 3D-printed using wood filament and then stained.

Accessories which add detail to the model are a variety of modified kits and scratchbuilt items but each has been chosen based on research and photographs from the period. For example, the Model T Ford is midnight blue as, contrary to popular opinion, black only became an option in 1913! The brewery truck is based on a vehicle at the Saurer museum and is modified from a Jordan Mack truck kit. The Kuoni horse-drawn wagon was scratchbuilt, based on a photograph from the history page of the Kuoni Transport website (who are still very much in business), but possibly my favourite is the dog cart for milk deliveries, typical of the period. Hotel coaches are brass/whitemetal kits, with detailing from Artitec and Weinert. The distinctive Hippsche Wendescheibe signal kits are from Bemo.

Above left
The chalet was constructed from balsa wood with some details 3D-printed.

Above
The chalet, barn, and chapel high on the hill look down on the loco shed.

Below
The balcony of the chalet is a great place for watching the trains.

Rolling stock

All rolling stock is proprietary, coming predominantly from Bemo, with some Ferro Suisse, STL, and D & R.

All three classes of steam locomotive which RhB used are represented – G3/4 (2-6-0 tank), G4/5 (2-8-0 tender), and Mallet tanks G2/2+2/2 (0-4-4-0) and G2/2+2/3 (0-4-4-2), as well as a rotary snow blower BB G 2x3/3 (0-6-6-0).

Coaches and wagons are of the period – balcony end coaches and baggage vans, with a variety of covered and open goods wagons with appropriate loads. The rolling stock has had detailing added and is lightly weathered to contribute to the ambience.

Control and electrics

The layout is DCC, with locos having a variety of decoders fitted; only the snow blower has sound.

Control is by Bachmann Dynamis Ultra hand controller and Dynamis RailController on a touch screen laptop. The general mode of operation is to control the track and accessories via the laptop and use the hand-held controller for locos. There are two infra-red receivers, one above the backscene and one in the fiddle yard so that coverage is maintained right round the layout.

A single power bus runs round the whole layout with dropper wires at every rail join, passing through aircraft-type plugs and sockets at the baseboard joins.

Point control at the front of the layout is by servos driven by two ESU Servo Pilots which also control the loco shed doors. The fiddle yard has an ESU Switch Pilot driving Peco side-mounted point motors, Peco track having been used throughout.

The turntable (also Peco) has a Meccano motor and gearbox which have simply been wired to the motor output of a loco decoder mounted under the baseboard. The lighting functions from this decoder are used to control LED lights in the station, engine shed, chalet, and church.

The turntable control is either aligned by Mark 1 eyeball or by programmed options in RailController. This does rely on the Meccano motor responding to commands in fractions of a second to get 100% accurate alignment; a stepper motor may be a future development to improve the accuracy.

When operating, route selection is either by individual point control on the touch screen schematic or programmed options, e.g. front loop to fiddle yard 1, 2, or 3, etc. which are single RailController commands via the touch screen. While locos can also be controlled from this, I prefer the handheld unit.

Conclusion and thanks

Building this layout has been a challenging project, with several thousand miles covered, literally. The research into the period, the social history, and the physical features needed to try and capture the detail for the layout has been very interesting.

Constructing the layout has also been a learning curve – my first venture into DCC, the use of servos, and developing CAD skills for 3D-printing, not to mention LED and SMD lighting, together with a range of materials and techniques I had read about but had no experience of using.

I have received positive comments from those who have seen the layout, and I feel I have achieved a lot of my objectives.

I could not have done this without the unwavering support and encouragement from my family and especially my wife, who has accompanied me to Hamburg, Filisur, Bergün, and all points in between while researching for this.

Membership of the Swiss Railway Society has been very helpful, as has the Railway Museum Albula at Bergün, with their bookshop and their willingness to answer e-mails with obscure questions written in poor German.

Next task – building the baseboards for *Neuburg 2013*!

Above
An overall view of the area around the station.
Two mixed trains are held waiting to pass a working in the opposite direction.
Photo: author.

Left
G3/4 2-6-0T 1 *Rhätia* arrives with a mixed local service while G4/5 111 waits on the station track and G4/5 104 (with original small tender) stands on the centre road.

Characteristic seasonal freight

Sugar beet

Peter Marriott shows how he modelled the sugar beet campaign on a diorama in HO.
Photographs by the author, unless noted otherwise.

Above
Sugar beet loaded into an Eaos bogie open wagon – a very common sight.

Approximately 38% of the land in Switzerland is cultivated farmland with most of the agriculture being done by small family farms. Around seven thousand farmers grow sugar beet on 18,000 hectares, and between October and December they are busy harvesting sugar beet and delivering it to rail loading sidings or directly to the two sugar processing plants at Aarberg and Frauenfeld.

During this annual three month sugar beet campaign, SBB Cargo moves around a one million sugar beets from various rail loading points and transports them to the sugar processing factories. In addition to making sugar, molasses and fodder are produced from the sugar beet at these plants.

During each sugar beet campaign, farmers haul their harvested crop on the road to designated loading sidings. In addition to the harvest from Switzerland, organic beets from southern Germany are moved by SBB Cargo from Schaffhausen to the sugar factory in Frauenfeld.

Sugar beets are processed in the Aarberg plant during the campaign from the end of September to the end of December. Each day, 8,500 tons of sugar beets are processed to produce 1,000 tons of crystal sugar, 200 tons of syrup, 200 tons of molasses, and 2,000 tons of pressed pulp remains as nutritious animal fodder.

Research

I visited Aarberg station in late November 2016 to watch the railway activity and was pleased to see that the factory and its sidings are visible from the station area. During my three hour visit a couple of SBB Cargo Tm235 diesel tractors were seen to be doing most of the shunting though a SBB Cargo Em923 in was also present in the main line loops. An SBB Re4/4^{II} stood nearby as Class 420 and 430 locos hauled trains to and away from the site, either singly or double-headed.

Since 2015 Schweizer Zucker AG at Frauenfeld has used a three-axle Krauss-Maffei M700C locomotive for shunting which was originally built in 1973 and has been modernised by LSB AG. The 66 ton loco, UIC number 98 85 5837 831-7 CH-ZAF, is equipped with a Deutz engine V8 and is fitted for remote control. See:

http://www.lsbag.ch/ueber-uns/news/detail/zuckerfabrik-frauenfeld.html

SBB Cargo sometimes publishes the sugar beet campaign timetable on its website (www.sbbcargo.ch); in 2016 it listed around thirty loading points between 5th October and 23rd December. The website usefully includes lists for earlier years. I was able to access the list simply by entering the word 'Zucker' into the search window.

Below
The unloading sidings at the Aarberg sugar processing factory.

Below right
In 2013 Trix announced a set (ref.23466) with four SBB Eaos wagons complete with sugar beet loads (by Duha) plus a tractor and trailer (by Wiking) and a laser-cut card kit for a loading facility.

When I visited Switzerland again in autumn 2017, I noticed that lots of the sugar beets were being moved in new grey containers on flat wagons carrying the name of ForstLogistik.ch.

Modelling

The main elements needed to represent the rail traffic are:
– a siding to accommodate the transshipment of the beets from a road trailer to open wagons.
– Eaos open wagons, some empty, some partially filled, others full.
– a loading facility.
– a tractor with one or more high sided trailers.
– farmers driving the tractors and assisting with the unloading while railway personnel direct operations in high visibility garments.

A few years ago Trix produced a useful set in HO (ref.23466) which included loaded Eaos wagons, a tractor with a trailer, and a laser-cut kit of a sugar beet loading facility. I have used this set as the basis for this feature. Other manufacturers produce SBB Eaos wagons in various scales, while loads of sugar beet for Eaos wagons can be made using a number of methods.

Loads for rail wagons

Cous-cous suitably painted could be used in HO or coarse sand in N. The wagon loads in the Trix set were made by for them Duha on pieces of polystyrene as a raised base; these could easily be made with scrap packaging material.

As an alternative to painted cous-cous, Juweela offer ready-made beet loads for 1:87, 1:45, and 1: 32.
www.juweela.de

The loads in the Trix HO pack are well made but the beets looked to be the wrong colour to me, so I initially repainted them with light brown acrylic paint. Once the first coat of paint had dried, to add more colour variety I mixed a thin wash of white and slate grey Woodland Scenics 'Earth Colours' and brushed it over the loads. I had noticed that in real life some of the beets are slightly damaged while being picked (see the accompanying picture) so to represent the part of the beet that has an exposed whiter centre I high-lighted small areas of the load with a little white. To give the last bit of colour, representing soil still left on the beet, I used two black felt tipped pens – one large one to rub over the surface and a smaller one to add some black dots.

Above
SBB Cargo tractor 232 207-1 shunts empty Eaos bogie open wagons at Aarberg, 29th November 2016.

Right
Shunting loaded Eaos open wagons at the Aarberg sugar processing factory.
Photo: courtesy SBB Cargo.

Below
A real sugar beet; it measures c.28 x 15cm.

Below
SBB Cargo Am843 diesel hauling loaded Eaos wagons in the early part of the campaign when the fields are still green.

Improving the appearance of the wagon loads

1

The supplied loads are well made but to me the beets looked slightly the wrong colour, so I repainted them.

2

Below: the load as it comes.
Above: after a coat of light brown acrylic paint.

3

For more colour variety I brushed on a thin wash of Woodland Scenics white and slate gray 'Earth Colours'.

4

After the first layer of brown acrylic plus a thin wash of the Woodland Scenics 'Earth Colours' mix.

5

I highlighted small areas with a little white 'Earth Colour' to represent the exposed parts of the beets.

6

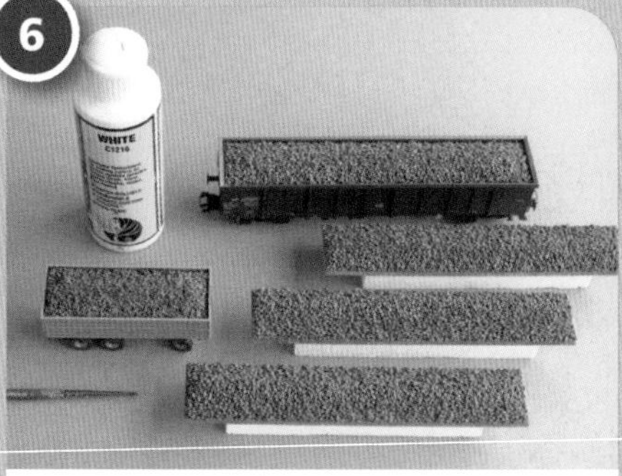

The four weathered wagon loads and the load in the trailer.

7

One of the almost finished loads.

8

To give a last bit of colour, representing soil still on the beets, I used black felt tip pens, a large one over the surface ...

9

... while a smaller one was used to highlight small parts on the beets.

10

The wagon loads supplied are raised on pieces of polystyrene.

11

A completed load after four stages of adding colour to the sugar beet.

12

The finished load in the road trailer.

Loading plant

The Trix set also features a laser-cut card kit for a loading plant. Using Noch 'laser' glue, the kit went together well. When making laser-cut card kits I am always careful not to get any adhesive on what will be a visible surface because if it is not quickly removed with a damp cloth it will leave a shiny mark.

The sequence of photos demonstrates how the structure was assembled.

The landscape in autumn

With the campaign running from October to December, consideration must be given to the colour of the grass, the weeds, the trees, and foliage to reflect the landscape at that time of year.

The later in the year you set any model, the fewer leaves will be on the trees and the more tired the grass and weeds along the sides of railway will have become.

The loading facility

1

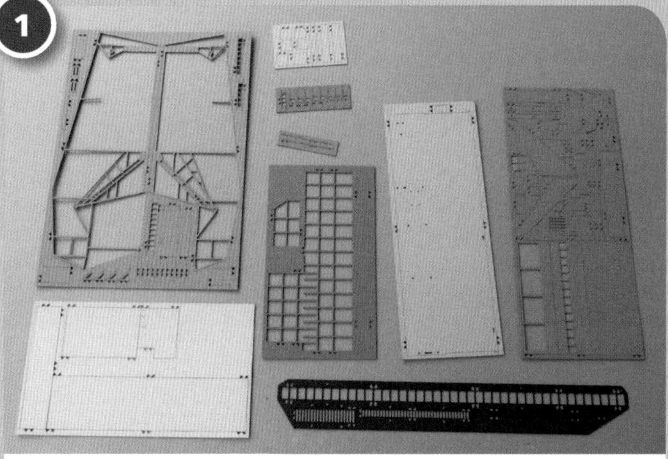

All the parts of the Trix laser-cut kit for a loading plant.

2

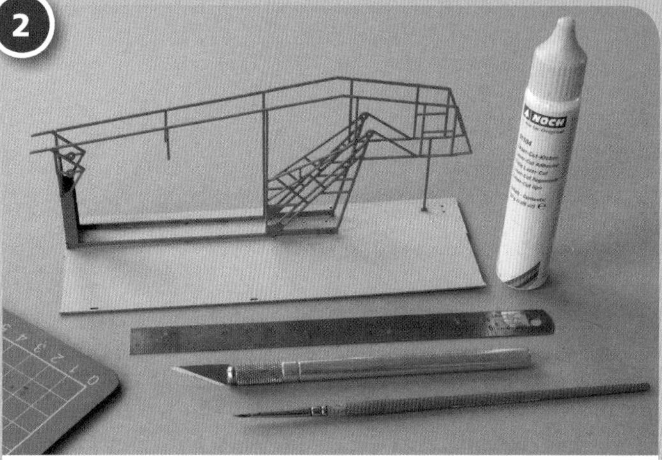

The main tools used – a craft knife, a steel ruler, Noch 'laser' glue, a self-sealing cutting board, and a small paint brush.

3

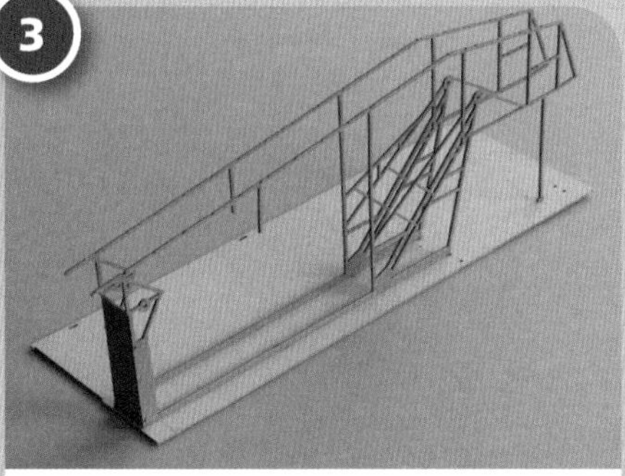

The kit comes with a card base into which the first three parts have been fixed with adhesive.

4

The weighbridge and other parts have been added. Revell matt varnish was used to hide any shiny spots of dried adhesive.

5

Juweela sell handy packs of sugar beet for HO, O, and 1.

6

The conveyor is taking shape and some of the Juweela beet has been glued to it.

7

8

The roof is corrugated iron sheets on a timber framework.

9

Roof parts fixed together.

10

The weighbridge.

11

The loading chute.

12

Loading an Eaos wagon.

13

Road side of the loading facility ready to be positioned on the layout.

14

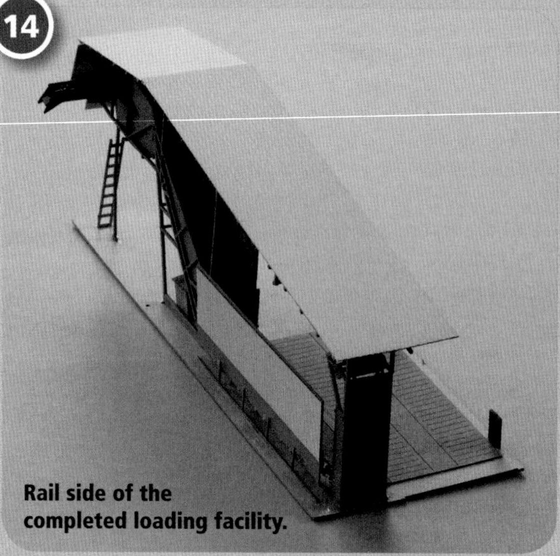

Rail side of the completed loading facility.

15

The tractor and trailer on the road side of the loading facility.

16

Loading two Eaos wagons.

This page
The sugar beet loading equipment adjacent to the station at Herzogenbuchsee near Langenthal with an Eaos wagon partially loaded, showing the location next to the large warehouse, the weighbridge for trailers, the hut for the staff, and the receiving hopper with conveyor belt. 31st October 2017.

Below left
A slightly different device loading sugar beet into Eaos wagons at Niederweningen. 26th September 2011.
Photo: David Aldis.

A possible subject to model, with interesting traffic

Herzogenbuchsee

Benno Wiesmüller proposes a plan for a busy junction in central Switzerland.
Drawings and photographs by the author.

The line from Bern to Olten through Herzogenbuchsee, and the link from there to Solothurn, was opened in 1857. The route was double-tracked from Olten to Herzogenbuchsee in 1874, and through to Bern in 1896.

In 1902, the five largest railway companies in Switzerland were amalgamated to form the Swiss Federal Railways (SBB – CFF – FFS).

An underpass was built at the southern end of the platforms in 1913.

In 1924, the wooden structure on the platform was renewed: the building had previously been used as an animal exhibition hall in Bern.

In 1925 the Bern – Olten line was electrified. The single track line to Solothurn was electrified in 1946.

A two track loco shed which had stood in the middle of the sidings area was demolished in 1950. The use of steam locos in this area came to an end in the 1960s.

Thanks to retired SBB station inspector Hans Schneeberger of Herzogenbuchsee for help with this article.

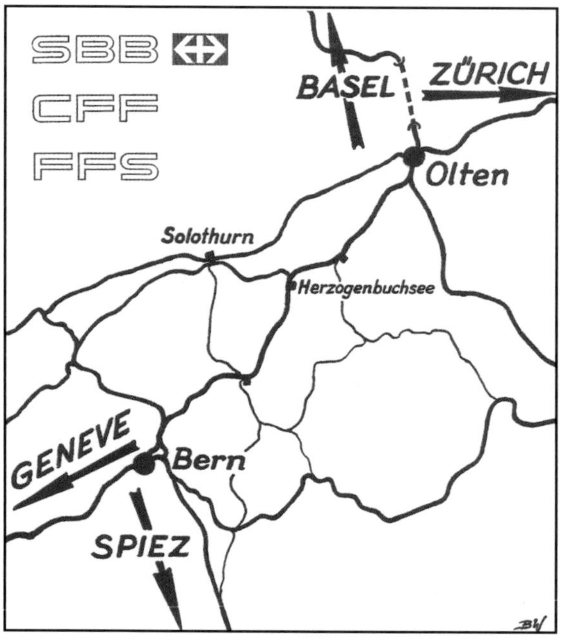

Above
Herzogenbuchsee station, seen from the north on 8th July 1998. On the right a shunter prepares to move a rake of hopper wagons.

Above right
Herzogenbuchsee station from the south. Note the Dt baggage driving trailer on the train. Forty of these vehicles were built between 1966 and 1971, numbered 920 to 959. An HO model was offered by EMB (Emmental Modellbau GmbH, www.emb-gmbh2.ch).

Right
Regionalverkehr Mittelland Re 456 143 of 1993 passing through Herzogenbuchsee with a freight. RM was formed in 1997 by merging the Emmental-Burgdorf-Thun-Bahn (EBT), the Vereinigten Huttwil-Bahnen (VHB), and the Solothurn-Münster-Bahn (SMB). In June 2006 it joined the BLS Lötschbergbahn to form the new BLS AG.

Right
Looking south. On the left is the goods shed and beyond that the station building. The ground signals for shunting date from the track alterations in 1979-1980.

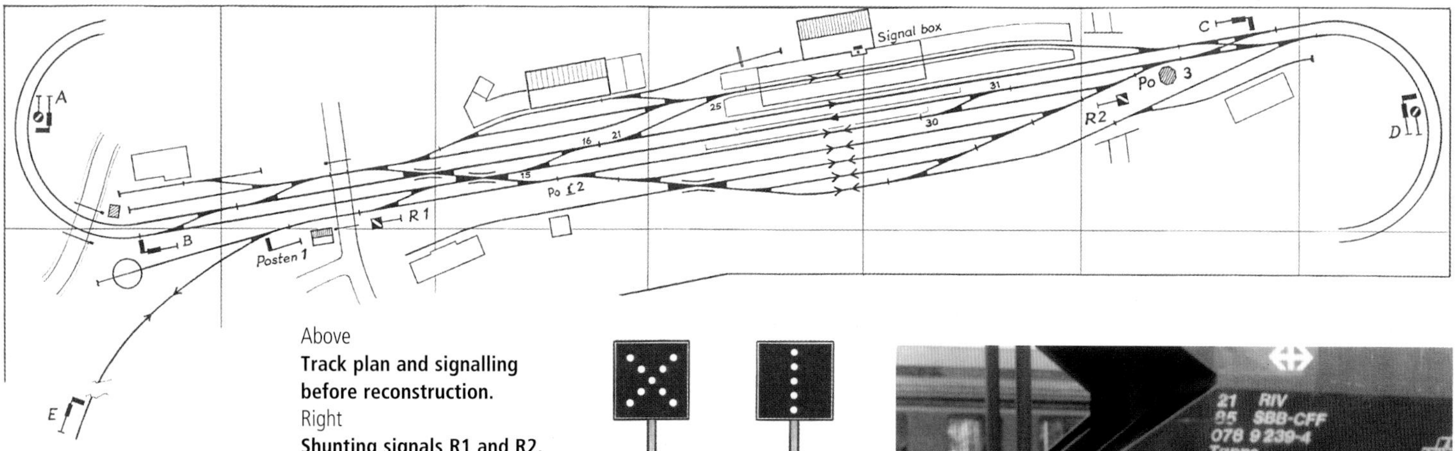

Above
Track plan and signalling before reconstruction.
Right
Shunting signals R1 and R2.

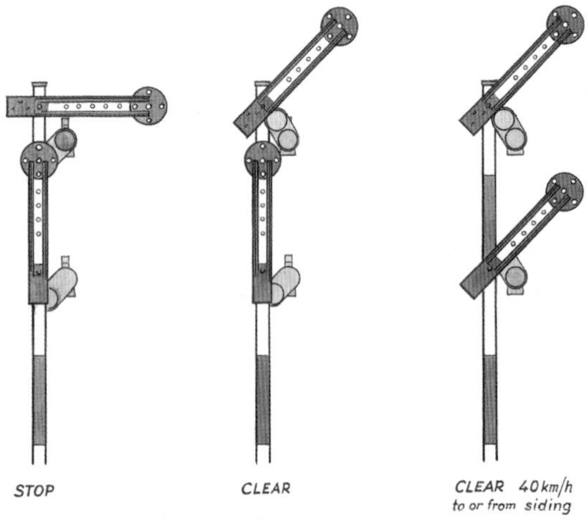

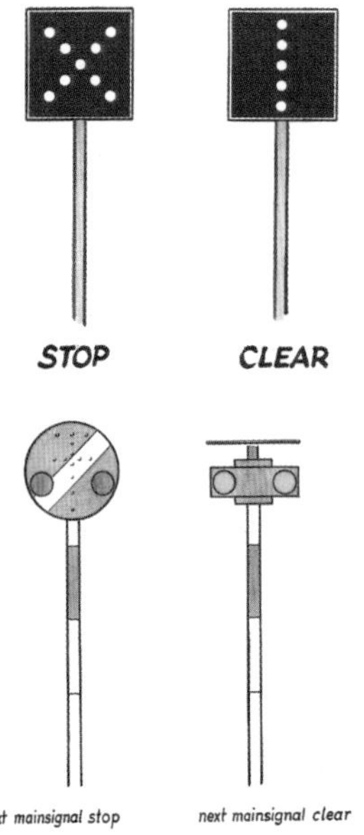

Right
An individual point lever for an adjacent point.

Left
The signal box in the station building during the summer of 1980, just before the building was modified and the new canopies added.
Hans Schneeberger collection.

The station was controlled from a mechanical signal box inside the station building. The points in the northern area were operated from Poste 1, those in the southern area by Poste 3. The semaphore signals and the two shunting signals R1 and R2 along with points 21, 25, 30, and 31 were controlled from the main signal box. Poste 2 was an open stand with single levers for points 15 and 16, and a

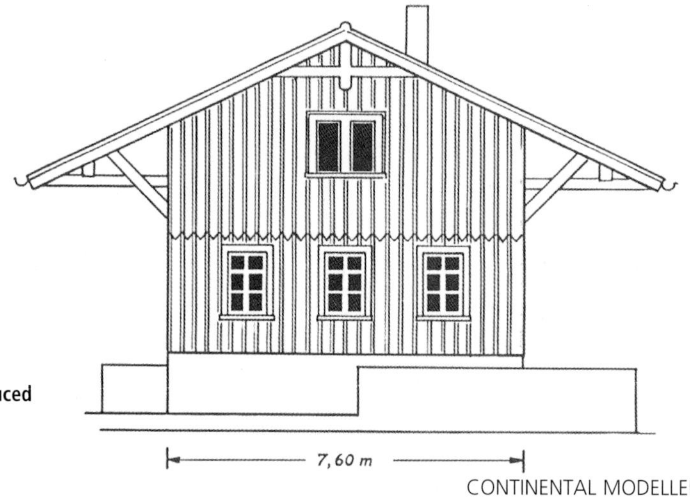

Right
The goods shed. Drawings reproduced to 1:160 (N).

telephone. Because there was only one starting signal for each direction, the order for the train to depart was given by the stationmaster.

In 1967 the semaphores were replaced by colour light signals.

In 1969 the level crossing between signals A and B was replaced by a road underpass.

In 1970 the level crossing by Poste 1 was replaced by a pedestrian underpass. Around the same time the station building was clad with stone slabs.

In 1979-1980 the track layout was rationalised.

The goods shed was closed in 1984. Until then, agricultural products were loaded here (e.g. potatoes and sugar beet) and cheese was despatched in refrigerated vans to places as far afield as Bremerhaven in northern Germany and Genoa in Italy.

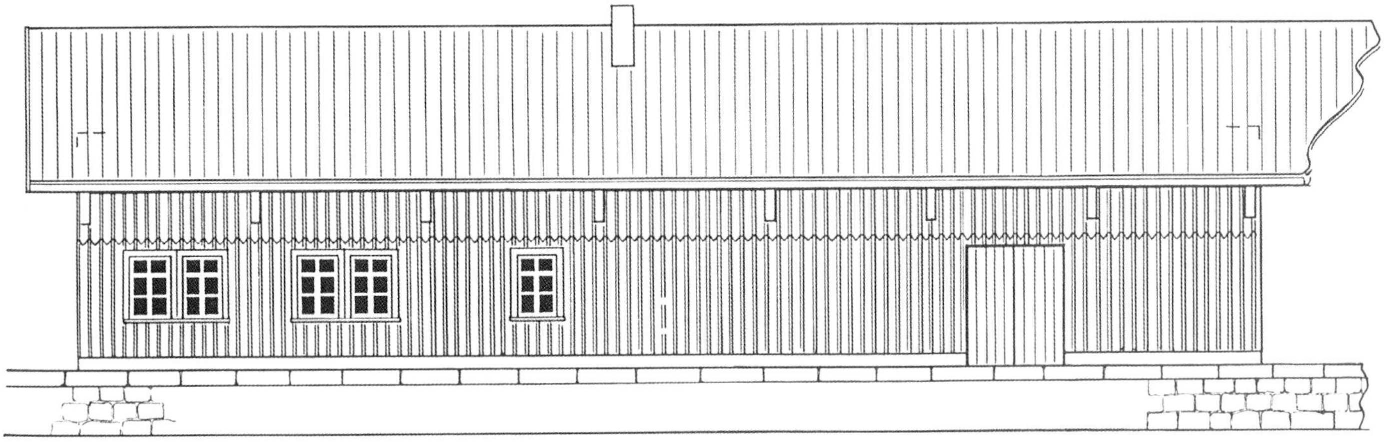

The cross-country line to Solothurn closed in 1992. Until the mid-1970s this route was operated by old Ae3/6 locos with three or four six-wheel coaches; they were succeeded by BDe4/4 railcars with driving trailers.

The Bern – Olten line remains an important artery, with north – south traffic via Basel and Spiez to and from Italy and east – west workings between Zürich and Geneva. Parts of the route have been increased to four tracks to raise capacity, in part with a parallel new high speed line since 2003/4.

The line has seen a number of international workings which allow the modeller to justify 'foreign' stock.

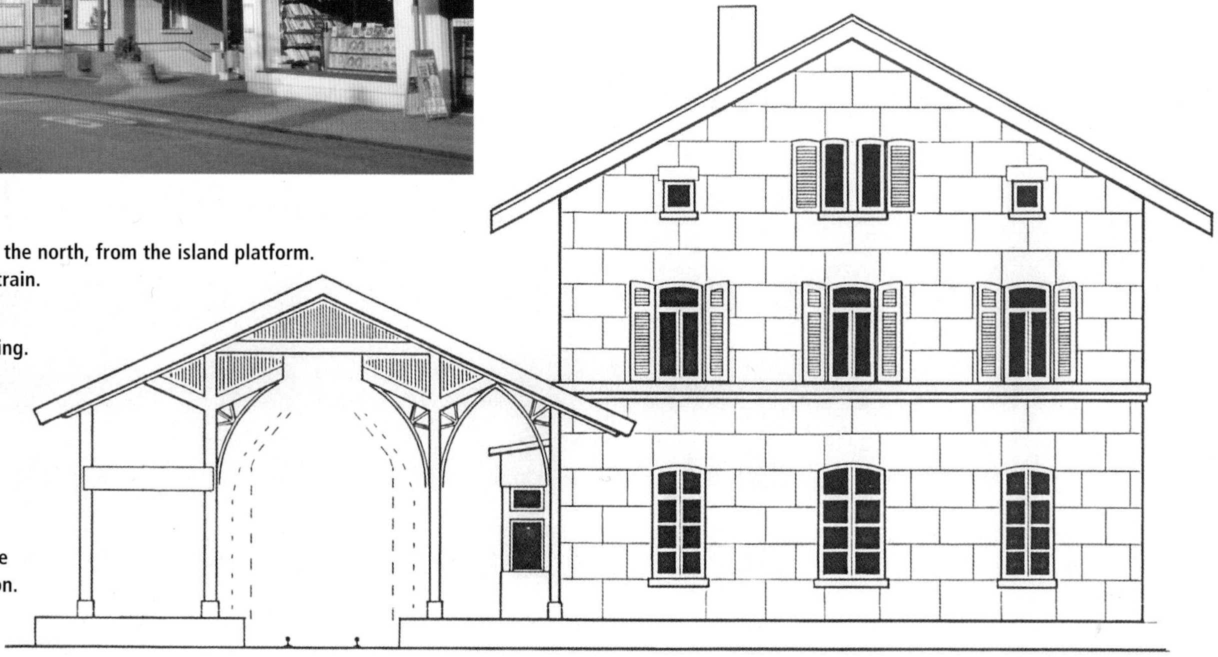

Top
The station building, from the north, from the island platform. Re 460 101-9 on a goods train.

Above
The road side of the building.

Right
The station building before the 1979-1980 modification. Drawings reproduced to 1:160 (N).

Berlin – Interlaken	ICE (Fleischmann or Roco)
Basel – Milano	Pendolino (Lima)
Zürich – Barcelona	Talgo (Electrotren)
Zürich – Paris	TGV (Jouef, Lima, or Mehano)

Suitable SBB locos include Ae3/6 (Fleischmann), Ae6/6 (Roco), Re6/6 (Lima), Re4/4 (Fleischmann), and Re460 (Roco). The BLS Re4/4 has been produced by Lima. Swiss specialists Hag have also produced most of these classes. Recently Piko have also started to make specials for the Swiss market, including the RBe4/4 (later RBe540) electric railcar and BDt driving trailer.

A wide selection of passenger and freight rolling stock suitable for different eras is now offered by many manufacturers, large and small. Older vans can be obtained from Märklin/Trix and Piko, and there are several small specialists in Switzerland such as AKU and Born.

Authentic Swiss stock has also been produced under the RailTop Modelle label (now only operating as a retailer) as well as by Tillig, Jägerndorfer, and LS Models.

These model suggestions are for HO; N gauge modellers are quite well served by major brands – Arnold, Fleischmann, Minitrix, and (in its time) Lima, as well as Kato.

Above
The station building, from the south, from the island platform.

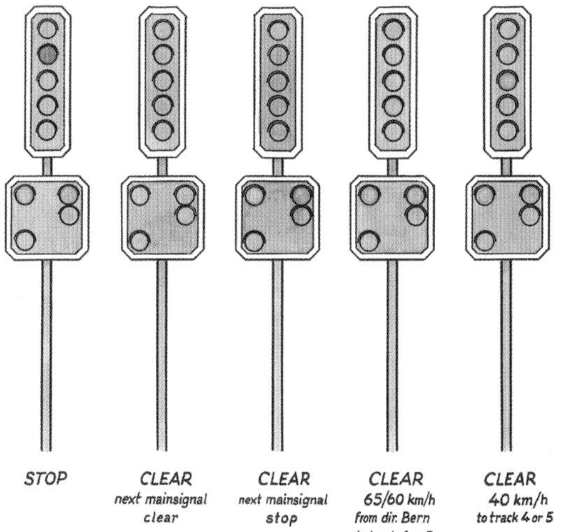

Above **Entry signals.**
Inset above **Ground signals.**

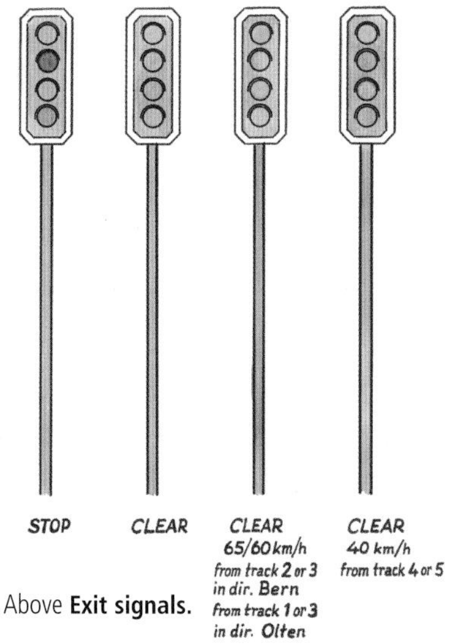

Above **Exit signals.**

Accurate models of the station and other buildings would have to be scratchbuilt, but this should not be too difficult. Sheets for the roofing are available from Vollmer and other firms; the wooden walls of the goods shed could be represented by Evergreen ref.4544 board and batten siding with a roof of Vollmer ref.6032. Dressed stone sheets for the loading dock can be found in the Faller and Vollmer ranges.

Swiss colour light signals are available from several companies, including Lemaco (refs.4081 and 4082, and 4093 ground signal) and Schneider.

Authentic catenary is readily available from Sommerfeldt.

The suggested layout plan (*right*) corresponds closely to the original; only the length has been reduced – the station would need about 13 metres in HO otherwise! The industrial sidings have also been simplified somewhat but still offer operating potential This enables a practical layout to be achieved in an area of around 6.35m by 2.5m.

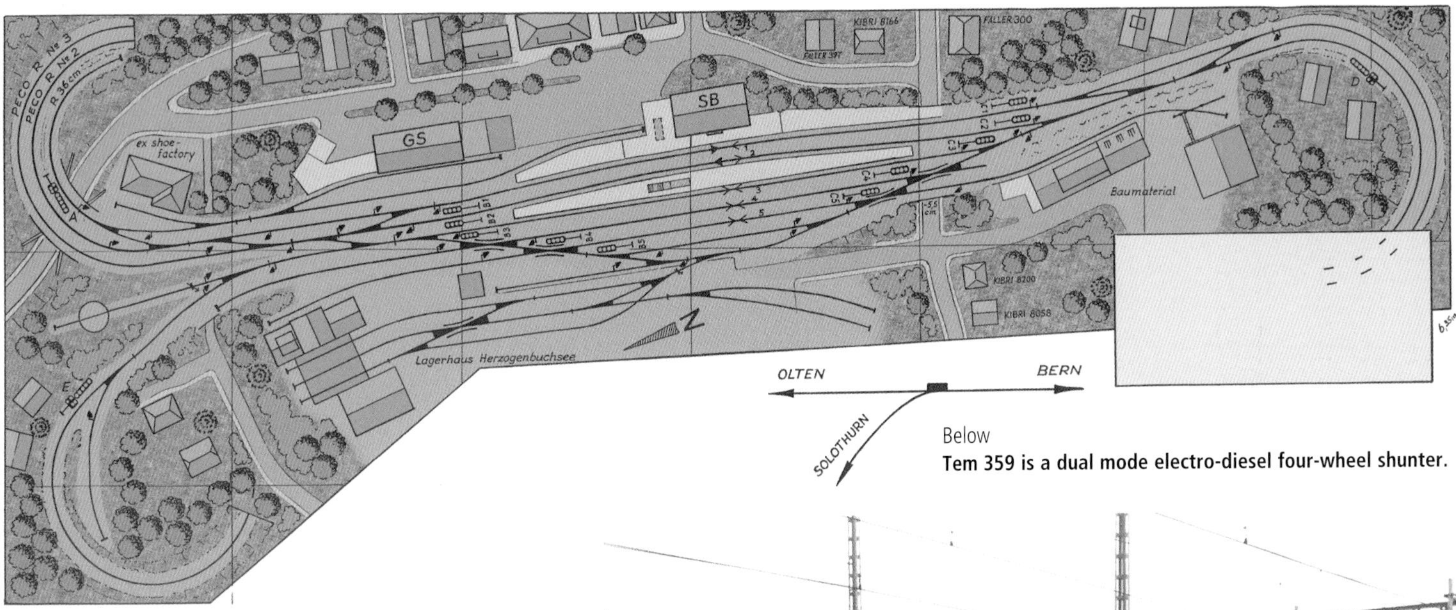

Below
Tem 359 is a dual mode electro-diesel four-wheel shunter.

Top left
The exit signals at the Olten end of the station. Re4/4II 11242 arriving with a train from Olten.

Above
The exit signals at the Bern end of the station; Re4/4II 11268 arriving. On the right is a building materials supplier's yard.

Far left
SBB Ae6/6 11417 *Fribourg*, from the first series delivered from 1955 for the Gotthard mountain route, with a goods train.

Left
SBB Re4/4II 11341 on a passenger service towards Olten.

Irgendwo

Dave Edwards describes his metre gauge layout, which was designed to be exhibited.

I started railway modelling seriously in the 1960s when I joined Stourbridge Model Railway Club, who were just starting to build a coarse scale O gauge stud contact exhibition layout. As I was a telephone engineer, it was my task to wire and solder all the studs on this layout. Eventually I was allowed to help with the scenery and all the other interesting jobs under the watchful eye of the layout foreman.

After a few years of taking this huge heavy layout around the country, we decided to build a smaller fine scale O gauge end-to-end layout which gave us the opportunity to attend many exhibitions over the following years.

When the club was forced out of its premises, a few of us got together to build various other exhibition layouts which kept us involved over quite a few years. I also visited many exhibitions helping out on O gauge trade stands until a few years ago.

Above
Ge6/6[II] 706 *Disentis/Müster* pulls away from Irgendwo with a passenger train formed mainly of older heavyweight steel coaches.

Photographs by the editor.

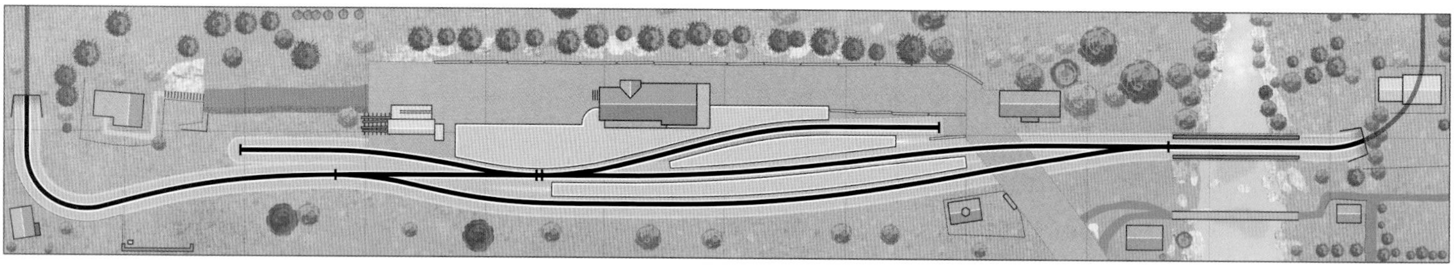

During a conversation in 2011 we were discussing all the new products now on the market for model railways, when someone suggested we ought to build an exhibition layout and find out how we got on with them. The next decision we had to make was what prototype to model. This should have been an easy decision, but we wanted to do something that was totally different to anything we had done before. My friend Mark Dale suggested German HOe narrow gauge, while I fancied doing some Swiss HOm metre gauge, so in the end we built both *Bertsdorf* (see CM January 2018) and *Irgendwo*. While *Bertsdorf* is based on a real location, *Irgendwo* is a fictitious village in the Canton of Graubünden somewhere between Chur and St.Moritz in the Albula valley served by the Rhätische Bahn.

Below
G4/5 2-8-0 108 hauling a train of historic stock approaching Irgendwo.

We needed to design the baseboards to fit into two medium sized cars, so the first thing to do was measure the space and work out the maximum length and height available. We eventually decided on a scenic section 12' long and 2' wide, with a backscene 21" high. The length was made up with two 4' and two 2' baseboards. These boards could then be packed one on top of each other to form box sections that could easily be transported. A fiddle yard large enough to hold twelve complete trains was constructed made up of three 4' sections which could be packed into another 'box'. Two 3'6" boards which feed the fiddle yard make up the last 'box'.

The next job was to design the track plan which needed to be simple to operate and yet interesting to the public. We decided on a single track with a passing loop in the station, with two loading sidings.

Above left and above
The left and right sides of the scenic section.

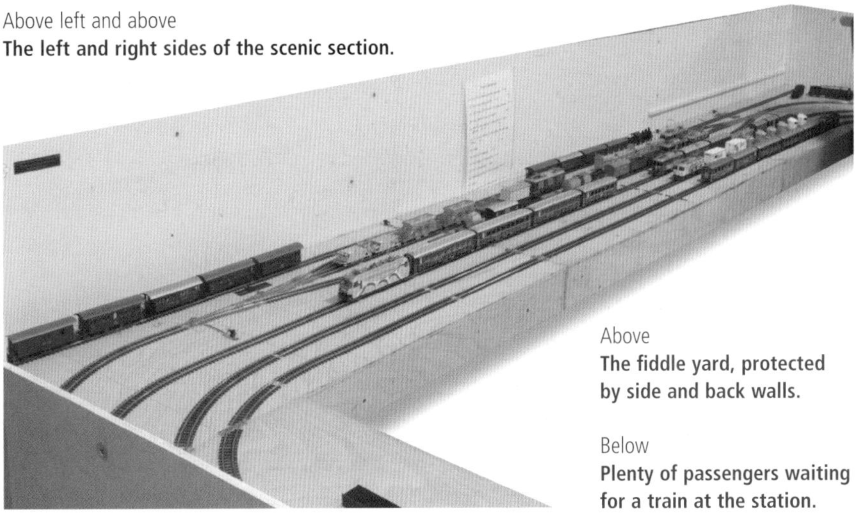

Above
The fiddle yard, protected by side and back walls.

Below
Plenty of passengers waiting for a train at the station.

Below
The layout at a glance – 1:
a Ge4/4^{II} collects timber wagons from the siding; Gem4/4 electro-diesel 802 is stabled with snow blower Xrotd 9213.

Above
Basic baseboard structure.

Below
Baseboard with scenery formers – this will be the waterfall.

Above
Laying track on the main baseboards.

Below
Landscape base in place. Construction photos by the author.

Above
Ge6/6[II] 706 *Disentis/Müster* crossing the bridge.

Below
The Post bus has parked next to the catenary switch frame.

Below
The layout at a glance – 2: the timber train has left.

The four main baseboards are of the open framed design made from L-shaped plywood formers whereas the other baseboards have the normal solid tops. Formers were cut from plywood for the scenery and fixed in place along with the track base. The formers were covered with chicken wire and Woodland Scenics lightweight hydrocal plaster which was painted ground colour.

The Peco track was then laid and wired so that initial testing could be done. The points are operated using Hoffman slow action point machines.

Below
The layout and all necessary accessories for an exhibition (we hope!) can be loaded into two medium sized cars.

Photos by the author.

Above
Ge4/4^{III} 644 *Savognin* with Viessmann advertising hauling a passenger train passes a goods consisting of bogie container flats and sliding side vans.

A sequence for operations was devised and tested to ensure that various train consists could be run as envisaged. Once this had been done it was time to carry on with the scenery.

Rock outcrops were produced using Woodland Scenics moulds, and the river was created using their products.

Above
The station building.

Above right
Now the passenger train has cleared the station, the goods train behind Ge4/4^{III} 643 *Vals* can depart. The small wayside chapel is hosting a stylish wedding.

Right
Ge4/4^{II} 628 *S-chanf* with a timber train overtakes the G4/5 2-8-0 and its special.

Left
Gem4/4 electro-diesel 802 trundles through the station with a works train.

Viafier retica

Above
Ge4/4^II 615 *Klosters* in RE-Power (Rhätia Energie) livery with a timber train.

Buildings were constructed from kits by various manufacturers and temporarily fixed in place and marked out ready for the various layers of vegetation to be applied using static grasses and other scatter materials.

The backscene was printed onto A3 sheets using photographs taken on various visits to Switzerland over a number of years.

Trees were made from commercial kits, supplemented with cheap firs to make up the bulk.

The next major task was installing the overhead catenary, from the Sommerfeldt range. A lot of research was undertaken to ensure the model was as close to the real thing as possible.

There are two control panels, the main one at the front of the layout and one in the centre for the fiddle yard; both use Modelex controllers.

The locomotives and rolling stock are mostly by Bemo.

Left
Ge4/4^II 611 *Landquart* in the 'login' promotional livery applied in 2017 rumbles past the chapel with a freight.

Below
Rebuilt Ge4/4^{I} 606 *Kesch* and Ge4/4^{II} 633 *Zuoz* double head a long freight.

MIB

Alan Pike explores the Meiringen Innertkirchen Bahn, a self-contained metre gauge line which might make an interesting and unusual model either at home or for a club.
Photographs by the author.

Above
Zentralbahn 110 003-1 at Meiringen ZB station, before the rebuild. 7th September 2009. The Innertkirchen line starts some way off to the left.

Left
One of the new Zentralbahn Stadler SPATZ (Schmalspur Panorama TriebZug) sets arriving at Meiringen. Tractors 171 203-3 (Te2/2^{III}) and 172 597-7 (Tm 2/2^{II}) will not be required to shunt coaches off this train! 12th September 2009.

Above
Meiringen Zentralbahn station, 8th September 2009. Stadler-built unit 130 001 on the Interlaken shuttle and 101 964-5 with a train for Luzern.

Below
Meiringen station, road side. 11th September 2009.

Early days

This short line in the Bernese Oberland is relatively little known even to the Swiss.

A concession was granted in 1926 by the Swiss government to operate a railway from a junction at Meiringen to Innertkirchen (sometimes still seen in the old form of Jnnertkirchen), a distance of 4.99km. It was planned to extend the line down the Aare valley some 8km to the village of Guttannen but this was abandoned on cost grounds.

A year earlier, the Kraftwerke Oberhasli A.G. (KWO, or Oberhasli Power Station Ltd.), who were constructing a large hydro-electric generating station at Innertkirchen, had put an industrial railway into service from Meiringen to serve the plant. It was, for obvious reasons, built to the same gauge as the erstwhile Jura – Simplon, later Swiss Federal Railways (SBB), and now Zentralbahn (ZB) metre gauge line from Interlaken Ost via Brünig-Hasliberg to Luzern.

Two steam locos were obtained from the Rhätische Bahn to work the line. Freight working began on 1st August 1926. In 1931 a battery-powered four-wheel tractor with twelve seats, No.3, was bought to provide a limited passenger service for employees. It was taken out of service in 1979 and sold to the Deutscher Eisenbahn-Verein at Bruchhausen-Vilsen where it is numbered T46.

In 1939 Schweizerische Industrie-Gesellschaft (SIG) supplied two larger four-wheel vehicles, numbered 4 and 5, again powered by batteries. These seated twenty-two passengers and operated both freight and the services for employees.

In 1946 approval was given for the MIB to carry the general public.

I travelled in one of the SIG units in 1975 – I think it was No.4 and in a blue and off-white livery at the time. The other was in store in the shed at Innertkirchen. The ride was not as rough as I had expected, probably because it seems the track had been improved prior to the granting of a renewal to the government concession in that year.

No.4 went to the superb Swiss Transport museum at Luzern in 1982 but No.5 is still on display at Innertkirchen

Above
Golden Panoramic Express hauled by ZB 110 003-1 approaching Meiringen. 10th September 2009.

Below
April 2010 – rebuilding the Zentralbahn station, showing the shell of the new island platform. Note the curving connection to the MIB.

KWO, although the two narrow gauge mining railway vehicles used in the construction, and probably maintenance, of the electricity works, one of which I recall was a people carrier, have gone to the transport museum.

Although the railway operation had been, technically, hived off from the parent KWO in 1946, little changed in practice. Improvement to the motive power had become essential. The light axle load, 9 tonnes, and only four-wheels meant that the adhesion capability of the battery railcars was no longer adequate.

Electrification

Electrification would be the answer but it was not easy. The chosen supply was 1,200V d.c. by catenary. There was no problem with the sections in the open but for 1,502m the line is in a tunnel running alongside the river Aare which at that point has cut a vertical sided slot in a massive rock outcrop. The vertical clearance is only 5m.

A novel solution was adopted. Two trams built by Fuchs in 1952, numbered 63 and 65, were bought in 1977 from the Oberrheinischen Eisenbahngesellschaft (OEG) in Mannheim. Each car seated 34 passengers and in addition to its good adhesion it was sprightly, with an authorised top speed of 65km/h. They were numbered 6 and 7 on the MIB and painted orange. Another OEG tram, number 68, was bought in 1978 as a reserve and kept in the works at Meiringen.

In the SBB works at Meiringen the cars were not only modified to satisfy Swiss practice but also fitted with diesel engines to provide power through the tunnel. There was a bonus – no overhead catenary was installed where the single connecting line to the SBB at Meiringen crosses a main public road, thus enabling the converted trams to work to and from the exchange sidings. No.6 was re-motored in 1998 with a larger diesel engine and worked as a tractor until scrapped in 1999; No.7 was broken up around 2001.

These days, a contact wire crosses the road and because of the widely different current between the ZB (15kV 16.66Hz a.c.) and the MIB (1,200V d.c.) isolating switches are necessary. Isolation was on the MIB side (as shown in the photo overleaf) but was moved across the road when station was remodelled in 2010.

Motive power variety

One great thing about modelling such a railway, apart from it being pretty compact, is the variety of motive power which has been used over time.

In 1988, Berner Oberland Bahn (BOB) ABDeh4/4 No.301 was hired to work freight, including *Rollschemmel* – metre gauge transporters carrying standard gauge wagons – from Meiringen to Innertkirchen. By this time, catenary was in place through the tunnel and the profile of this railcar was sufficiently small. It remained in standard BOB cream & brown livery.

In 1997 the MIB obtained 1961-built Be4/4 No.74 from Regionalverkehr Bern – Solothurn, in blue & white livery, and numbered it 9. It was replaced by No.11 in 2005. Plans to restore it as a historic vehicle for the RBS failed in 2007 due to the high cost of asbestos removal.

No.11 was Chemins de Fer du Jura BDe4/4 No.604. It retained its red & white livery and is still on the books as a reserve when the new No.8 is not available.

By 1996, as a result of some engineering works in the tunnel, a brand new railcar, Be4/4 No.8 was delivered by the Swiss Stadler works with a wide and low profile. It seats 40, has an authorised top speed of 75km/h, and rides well. The original livery was red & grey. It was later named *Oberhasli/ Innertkirchen* and in 2009 carried a basically light blue livery covered in advertising.

Gem4/4 No.12 is former Chemins de Fer du Jura luggage railcar De4/4 No.402 dating from 1952, acquired in 2010 and rebuilt with the addition of a diesel engine for track maintenance trains. It was operational in 2011.

Tractor Tm^{II} 10 was former Brünigbahn Tm^{II} 980, obtained in 2000. It was built in 1959 as SBB 709; since 2011 it has been preserved by La Traction based at Pré-Petitjean on the Chemins de Fer du Jura.

A second-hand Be2/6 two car articulated electric train set with a top speed of 80km/h was bought from Transports Montreux–Vevey–Riviera in 2016 and is being adapted for the MIB, but is not in service yet.

X 10 is a snowplough (not powered), which would be a wonderful subject for a skilled modeller.

Above
ZB 101 966-0 by the shell of the new island platform at Meiringen. 26th April 2010.

Below
The former Hotel Terminus opposite Meiringen Zentralbahn station. 9th September 2009.

Above
Approaching the MIB station from the ZB station. The level crossing sign protects the single line connection for freight and stock access across the road.

Above
MIB Be4/4 No.8 at the 'platform' at Meiringen MIB.

Steam has returned to the line. I enjoyed my first run along the MIB by steam in 1988, hauled from Interlaken Ost to Innertkirchen by G3/4 No.208 built for the SBB Brünigbahn by Swiss Locomotive and Machine Works (SLM) at Winterthur in 1914. This locomotive is adhesion only but another which has run similar special trains is also from the Brünigbahn, HG3/3 No.1067, built by SLM in 1910, which is rack and adhesion. (Most of the ZB line between Meiringen and Giswil is rack fitted.) These steam runs with trains of vintage carriages are a regular feature on the ZB in summer months and at almost any time for groups. It is to be hoped that steam will continue, despite the loss of the turntable at Meiringen, long into the future.

Along the line

Let us take a ride along the line as it was until April 2010.

Things are changing at Meiringen with extensive rebuilding of the station and remodelling of tracks which will result, *inter alia*, in the removal of the turntable and the MIB trains running into one face of the new island platform. In the diagram, I have interpreted the data currently available as well as I can. One benefit to the modeller is that it now provides an interesting and natural starting point.

Despite what has been written elsewhere, it is easy to find the MIB for those arriving by the ZB. Face the dead end of the ZB at Meiringen and you may still see the railcar awaiting you in its station, reached by walking up the curving approach road to the ZB station and turning right. The link between the ZB and the MIB is on a steep gradient and the line crossing the road can be seen. It takes less than five minutes – for the young and fit!

Looking down the MIB, to the left is the old wooden station building with lettering in the old form. The service train usually departs from the siding off the 'main line'.

Be4/4 No.8 was waiting to provide the mid-morning service from Meiringen on 12th September 2009 and was packed with passengers, including many standing. This was the day on which the annual ceremony was to be held in Innertkirchen to welcome the cows in all their finery on their return from mountain pastures to winter quarters.

The railcar pulled away with nothing more daunting to face than the ruling gradient of 1:50, apart from a few hundred metres to the KWO works near the end of the line.

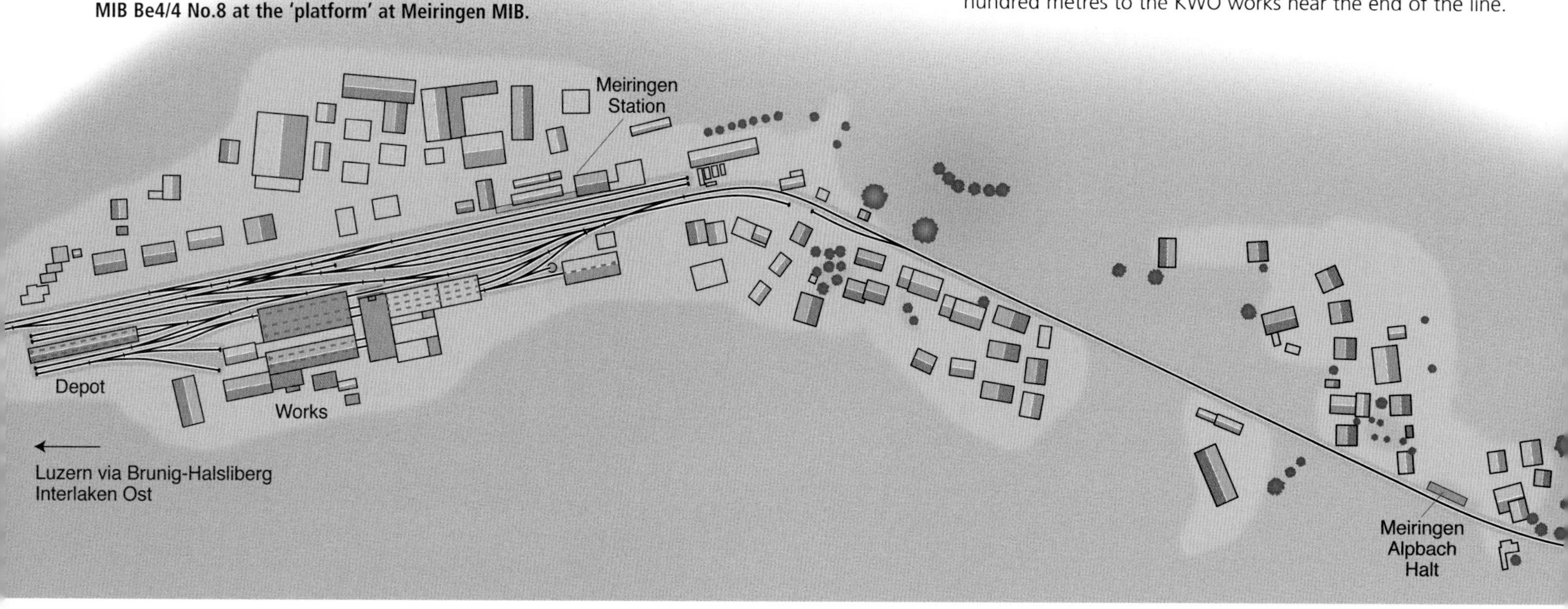

Above
Meiringen MIB looking towards Innertkirchen. Note the platform/mounting blocks. The gentleman is noted Swiss rail expert and author Hans Wägli.

Right
The complicated electrical isolation at Meiringen MIB where the 1,200v d.c. meets the ZB 15kV 16.66Hz a.c.

Above
The station building at Meiringen MIB. (Innertkirchen was formerly Jnnertkirchen, hence the initials M.J.B.).

Left
The station name in the old form under the side window of the station building.

All photos on these pages – 26th April 2010.

The route is on flat meadowland following the general line of the river Aare. After about 700m, a modern halt at the left, Alpbach, serves the outskirts of Meiringen. On the right the river can now be seen gradually getting closer as it approaches the gorge.

There is a small wooden halt on the left named Aareschlucht West serving not just a few local houses but also people who have walked the spectacular path along the other side of the gorge. They may use a long footbridge spanning the river, to spare themselves the walk the rest of the way back to Meiringen.

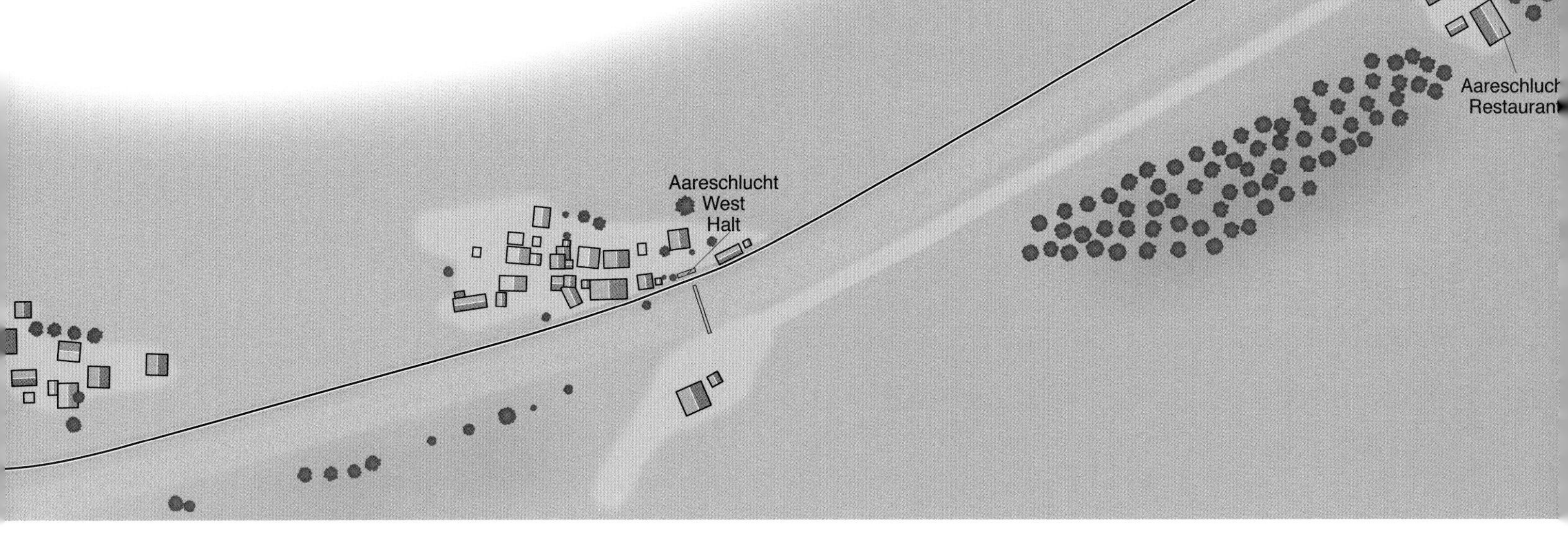

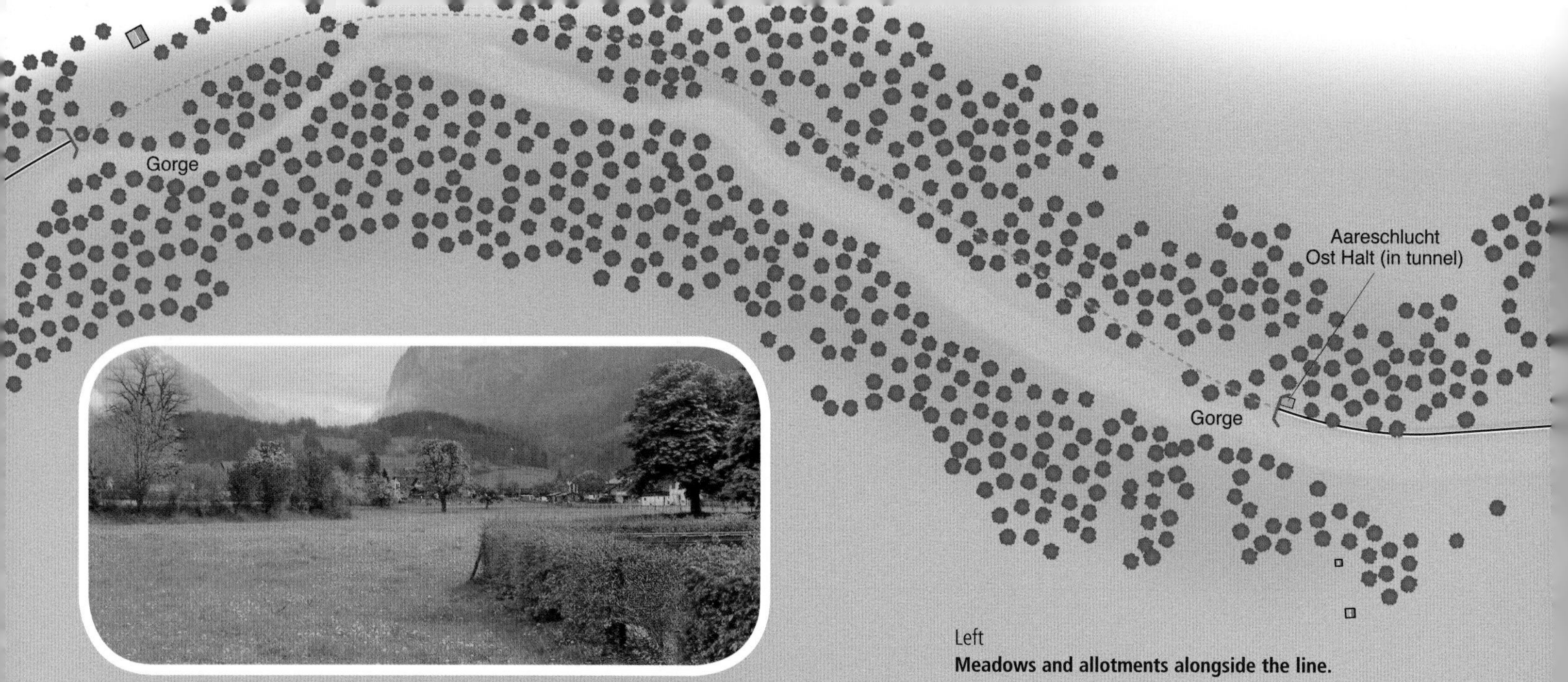

Left
Meadows and allotments alongside the line.

Above
The approach to Unterwasser halt, looking towards Innertkirchen.

Below
MIB Be4/4 No.8 about to cross a tributary of the River Aare at Unterwasser.

The railway then runs in a tunnel, 1,502m long, in which it remains hidden from, but close to, the river throughout its length. Aareschlucht Ost halt is actually inside the tunnel and as it seems from my experience that the train rarely stops there, when on the train one has to keep a sharp look out to spot it.

After leaving the tunnel there is open meadow to the right and a steep wooded slope to the left. The train slows as the driver checks to see if there are people from the nearby works or passengers on the train wanting to use the tiny halt at Unterwasser. If so, the train stops across the small road which follows a tributary of the Aare. Immediately after setting off, the train crosses the rushing stream on a through truss bridge of the Warren type and almost at once enters a short, sharply curving, tunnel through a rock outcrop. The road skirts this but closely follows the line all the way to Innertkirchen Post.

On the left of the line, one can see where the tarmac of a lane was extended to the trackside identifying the site of what was once called 'Innertkirchen Hof', presumably after the nearby hotel. The old wooden station building has gone, replaced by a minimalist bus shelter some 100m further on to the right of the line by a busy road crossing and called grandly 'Innertkirchen Post'.

On this particular journey, the railcar emptied here as people set off towards the village some 300m distant there to find a variety of stalls and tents providing a range of liquid and solid refreshment, especially local cheeses. It is a pleasant place with spectacular mountains rising nearby but also surrounded by flat, lush meadows on which the cows spend time before the snow comes and in the spring before returning to the mountains.

The train continues some 300m to the rather sprawling end of the line with no station building, just a sign on a warehouse wall, a clock, and a timetable: simple and effective, but there is little shelter for any passenger. It is not the absolute end of the line but all passenger services terminate here.

The supplementary diagram shows the track as it was before it was simplified and the works buildings were enlarged necessitating the removal of two loops. It can best be understood from the photographs.

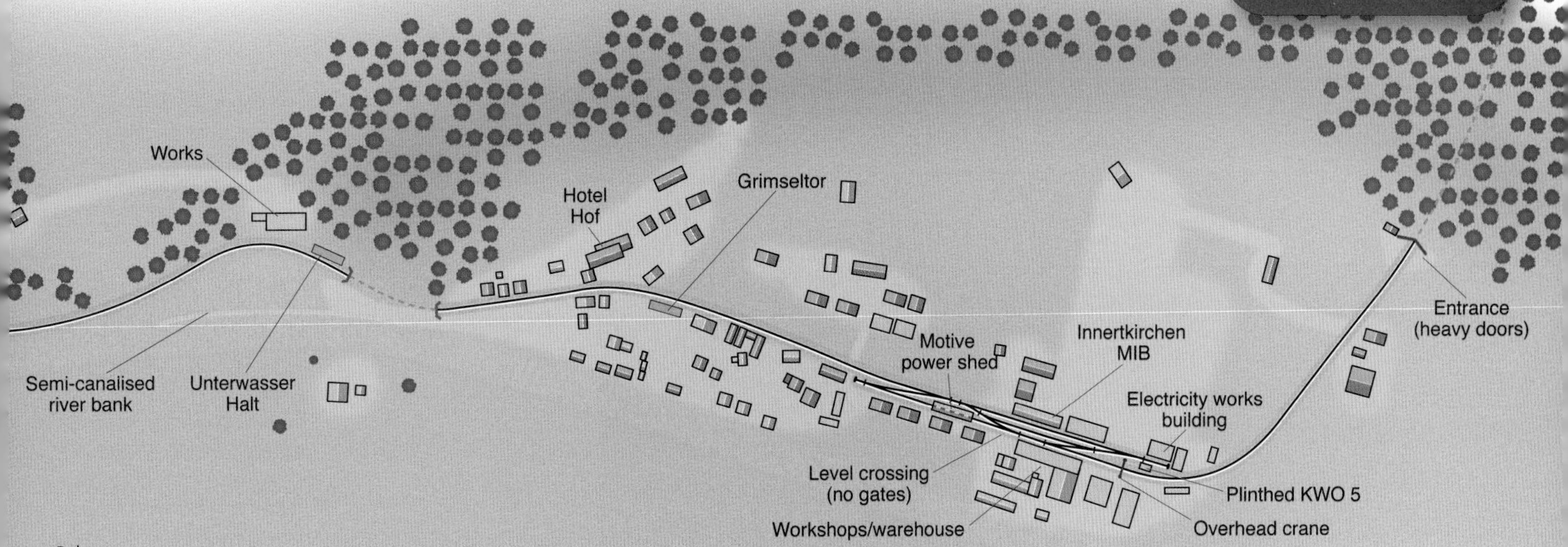

Below
The curved tunnel east of Unterwasser. ***All photos on these pages taken on 26th April 2010.***

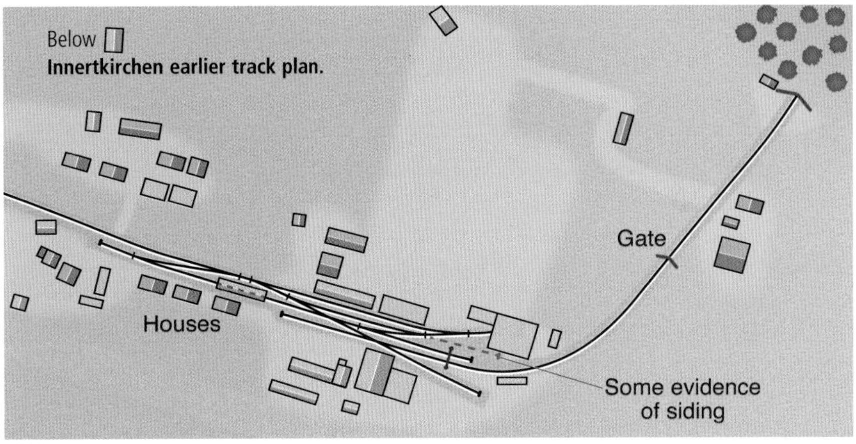

Below
Innertkirchen earlier track plan.

Below left
Innertkirchen Hof halt is simply denoted by the row of kerb stones.

Below
Hotel Hof & Post, Innertkirchen.

The line does not end here. The plan shows that one of the tracks curves sharply around the end building and continues for some 500m set into the surface of a good private road which leads to a large and very solid door in the mountainside. The road is clearly well in use but there is less evidence of regular rail traffic. It may be that this was the entrance to

Left
Innertkirchen KWO, looking back towards Meiringen. 25th April 1997. On the left is Bem4/4 No.6, formerly OEG No.63.

Below
Innertkirchen KWO, looking back towards Meiringen. 25th April 1997. The connecting line to the siding behind the shed was removed some time between 1997 and 2009.

Foot of page
The old warehouse and offices, Innertkirchen KWO. 26th April 2010. X 10 is a small snowplough.

the workings in days past and where the narrow gauge line ran, probably from exchange sidings at Innertkirchen KWO.

An unusual but easy walk back to Meiringen

If you are fit, do not take the train back, for here is one of the more unusual walks in Switzerland – and on the flat.

Walk back alongside the line from Innertkirchen Post, and past the curved tunnel. Across the meadow to the left you can see the path leading to the Aareschlucht. There is a ticket office where for a small fee you can enter a wonderland, a path cut into the vertical side of the gorge, sometimes diving into a short tunnel and then suspended on timbers out over the rushing waters. Looking up, especially if the sky is blue, gives a curious sense of the power of water conquering rock.

At the end of the gorge, just under a mile long, it is an easy wander back to Meiringen in its charming setting among the mountains. It is of course also famed for its association with Sherlock Holmes, whose statue and museum can be found in the main street.

Below
Young travellers wait at the limit of passenger services, seen over the shoulder of the driver of Be4/4 No.8. 26th April 2010. Stabled in the yard are snowplough X 10 and tractor Tm^{II} 10. Note railcar old No.5 on display in the distance.

Ideas for a layout

The individual modeller may well find that the Innertkirchen end of the line will satisfy both artistic and operational needs. The tunnel portal can be the entrance to the fiddle yard which, if you can ignore the 'bus shelter' station, could contain the stock of trains for any chosen period of the line's post-war existence: there seems to have been little change to the surroundings. It is also possible that if the village is to be part of the model, the railway could be brought to the front of the baseboard, transferring the village to the opposite side of the line.

For a club, both ends of the line could be modelled using the tunnel portal at the Meiringen end as one boundary and the public road dividing the MIB from the ZB as the other. However, instead of the line connecting the two railways passing across the road, the road should cross the line on a bridge which conceals the entrance to the fiddle yard. This, of course, would be suitable only if the period were to be before mid-2010.

The rebuilding of the ZB station gives the opportunity to present this end of the line in a different way. The plan attempts to retain the essential elements of the new station.

However, access to a fiddle yard could pose a problem as the line towards Interlaken Ost and to Giswil/Luzern heads straight out into open country. A curve, right or left, into a fiddle yard may be the only solution but backdrops with distant mountain scenes would add height and help to obscure this yard.

Sources

Most of this article is based on notes made during various visits over more than thirty years, but I must also acknowledge help from the following publications:

Schienennetz Schweiz (Wägli)

Lokomotiven and Triebwagen der Schweizer Bahnen – Band 3 (Willen)

Tramways and Light Railways of Austria and Switzerland (Buckley)

Triebfahrzeuge der Schweiz (Stolz)

Above
BOB ABDeh4/4 No.301, hired to the MIB for freight, at Innertkirchen on 13th October 1988. Note the more complicated – and interesting – track layout, with two double slips.

Right
The modern warehouse at Innertkirchen KWO. 26th April 2010. Note old railcar No.5 on display in the distance.

Left
The approach to the power station door in the mountain.

Below
The power station door in the mountain. 26th April 2010.

On the metre gauge Rhätische Bahn

The Andeer line

Derek and Julia Boswell explain the design considerations, the concept of operation, and the novel baseboard construction of their innovative HOm layout.

Photographs by the authors.

The wonderful thing about railway modelling is that there are so many facets to the hobby. For example, some seek to recreate childhood memories, others bring to life a long lost prototype complete in every detail. Whether it is diorama, a 'tail chaser', or 'basement empire', a layout will seek to fulfil many different interests and goals, ultimately providing fun and satisfaction. The many interests and skills of individuals and groups are reflected in pages of magazines such as CM. These can provide a great source of inspiration and encouragement. The enthusiasm which greets the realisation that "I can do something like that" is, however, often tempered by the realities of time, space, facilities, and finance (amongst others). But this should never stop us seeking ways of turning those dreams into reality.

The availability of layout design programmes on computers has taken armchair modelling to a whole new level. The challenge is to match the dream, the potential, and the reality. If we are to venture out of the armchair, the design parameters need to be worked out first or the result can be a waste of time, money, and that most important commodity – enthusiasm.

Everybody has different dreams and ideas of what they want in a layout. In the same way we all have different constraints that will affect the end result. After much thought, we decided on the main things we wanted from a layout.

Requirements

The Andeer line is an attempt to fulfil the dream of a large layout based on prototype practice where operations are the key factor. Building a model of an actual prototype was not high on our list. We were more interested in a system approach where the trains go from somewhere to somewhere else via a number of other locations rather than a 'theatre' approach where the trains come on stage from the wings (fiddle yards), do their acting (shunting), and then depart back to the rest of the world 'off stage'.

The layout is based on the prototype of the Rhätische Bahn in Switzerland, which has a variety of train formations, some mixed, which offer interesting shunting potential. Some of the stations may bear a passing resemblance to certain ones on the Bernina line between St.Moritz and Tirano. They are not, however, faithful reproductions but seek to capture the operational essence and possibility of the prototype. Whilst Andeer is a real town in Graubünden, it has never actually been served by the RhB, though a line was planned.

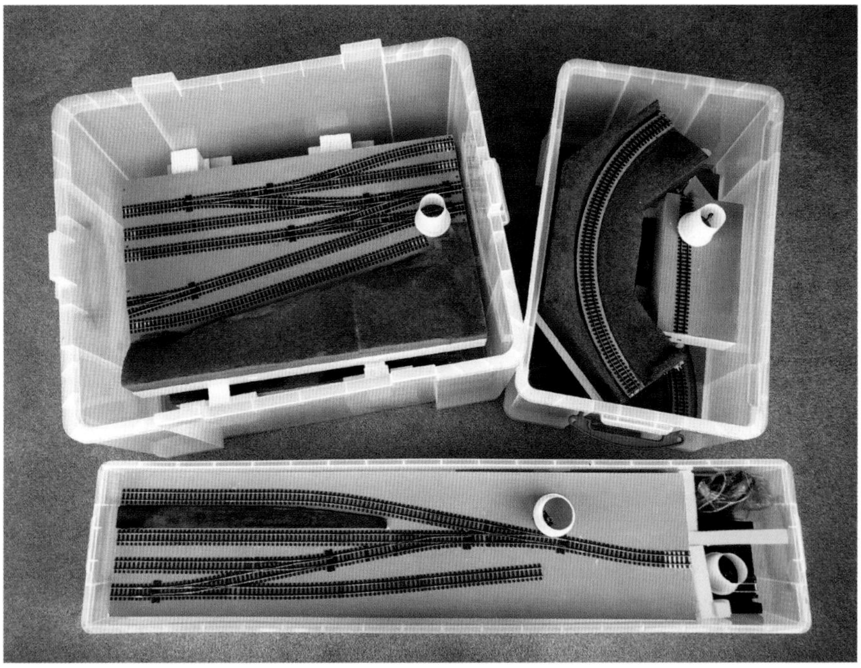

Above

The layout is stored in a variety of 'Really Useful' plastic boxes. Fitted with lids, they are stackable and give protection for transport. They have the advantage of being right-angled rather than tapered at the bottom.

Top left – 145 litre box.

Top right – 65 litre box.

Below – 77 litre, sold as a 'Christmas tree box'.

These were the first boxes we came across and bought, so the stations were designed this size because we had them. As it turned out, St.Moritz, Ospizio, and Samedan (the fiddle yard) all fitted quite well.

The white plastic cups help to protect the fixed colour light signals.

We also wanted something that would be adaptable to the number of people available to operate on any given occasion and set up location. We have discovered that the social side of operations can bring as much pleasure as the construction phase.

We also considered the possibility of exhibiting – if any shows would have us. Meeting fellow modellers and sharing different ideas and approaches is something that we have enjoyed in the past with other people's layouts.

Practicalities

Apart from lack of time, financial considerations, and technical ability, which were all key factors in the eventual design, one of the constraints we face is that we live in a flat, with no permanent place for the layout. Storage space is also at a premium, and furthermore access is via a circular staircase which limits board size and weight – also an important factor to consider in the future as we get older.

Also, we have no access to traditional woodworking facilities (garage, shed, or workshop). This meant that all construction would have to take place within the flat.

Following research into modular concepts such as FREMO (European) and FREE-MO (USA), plus others, the idea was born for a modular layout which could be set up easily in different configurations and packed away quickly. Normally it is put up in the main room but there is a limit to the amount of time we can forego complete access to our living and dining area. (This is very much a joint effort!)

Our first attempt at a layout facing these challenges used Styrofoam as a basis for small baseboards that fitted in to a range of 'Really Useful Boxes' for storage. It was designed to rest on tables – including the dining table. We used Tillig ballast bed set track, and the Kato style rail joiners used on this provided a means of linking boards without the need for access for tightening nuts and bolts. The weight was all taken by the tables. This also meant that the baseboards could be joined and separated easily and quickly. However, limitations in track geometry and robustness meant that further developments proved difficult. This layout pointed the way forward by using tables as a flexible base in terms of height and area, with small baseboards providing adaptability and ease of storage.

Having used Peco track on previous layouts we have always been impressed by the quality of the product. Living just along the coast from the factory also provided an incentive to overcome the challenges of using Peco track in this application. The two main issues were attaching flexible track to foam on a consistent curve, and joining and aligning baseboards. Track pins proved an unsuitable method of attaching flexible track to Styrofoam on anything other than a gentle curve. Whilst adhesives proved robust, accurate alignment at the end of baseboards allowing universal placement in a modular set up proved elusive.

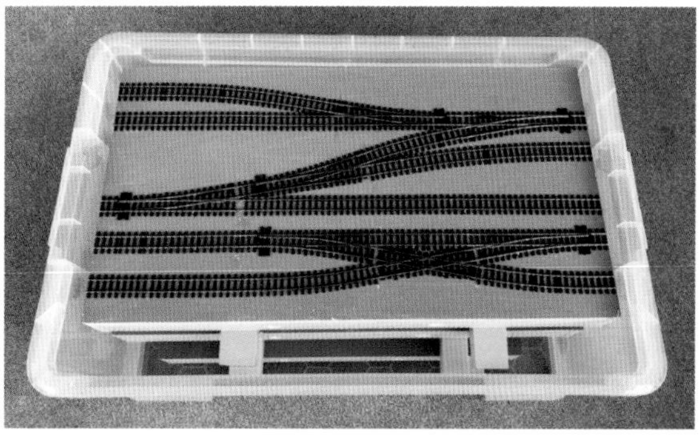

A chance conversation about estate agents' boards led us to a product called 'Foamalux Light'. This is a solid board available in 3mm, 5mm, and 10mm thickness which can be cut either by hand or a variety of power tools, including a router. This provided the solution to the curved track issue. Pins could be used to hold the track in place with the end of the rails being attached to copper-clad sleeper strip. Additional benefits include the foam's ability to take screws for the attachment of point motors and electrical equipment.

The alignment and joining issue was solved by the use of 20mm diameter magnets and board alignment dowels. The main purpose of the magnets is to prevent the boards moving apart. All the weight of the boards is taken on the tables.

We continued with the use of tables allowing flexibility in layout assembly and the 'Really Useful Boxes' for storage and transport, including all the control equipment and stock.

Above left
Our standard storage box is the 64 litre capacity and this determined the board dimensions and track radius for the 90° corners.
To make best use of available space, smaller straight boards have been designed to fit in the gaps.

Above
The boxes are transparent so a printed information sheet with large bold letters shows through the box lid providing contents and packing details.

Below
The layout stacked for storage. Normally the boxes would live around the room rather than all together in the corner – to improve the aesthetics, they can be covered with a cloth when we have visitors. They also make handy bedside tables and lamp stands!

Below
The largest box in the range is the 145 litre. With published internal dimensions of 710mm x 545mm x 400mm dictating the widest baseboard possible, the Pontresina station throat pointwork was worked out to fit two boards, one for each end of the station. We did first check that these boxes would go through the doors of the flat!
The one major piece of scenery, a river scene at the end of Pontresina, also fits into this box size.
Whilst the boards could have been wider, access for fingers to lift the boards out is essential – you cannot tip a layout out of a box!

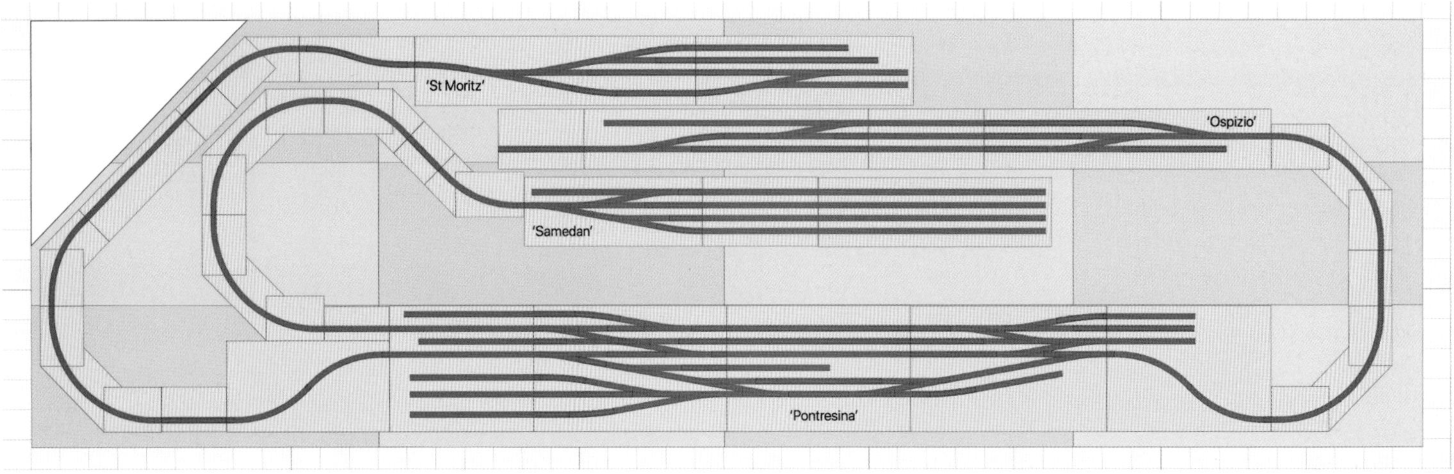

Above
The first plan.

Below
The cut pieces of Foamalux set out in the original 15'6" x 4'6" table configuration. Sometimes when something is laid out full size a better arrangement can be made – one advantage of a modular system. These board tops have since been re-used in the new arrangement.

Design

Using the internal measurements of the boxes, plans were drawn up for stations based on those on the Bernina line. These included part of St.Moritz, Pontresina, Ospizio Bernina, and Tirano. Each one provides a source or destination for a variety of traffic, and operations are based on those of the prototype. This means we can run a wide range of train types such as expresses (with suitable locomotive changes), passenger services, with freight attached as required, and heritage specials. All the rolling stock is Bemo and a wide range of liveries representing various periods may be on show. An Allegra multiple unit has not made an appearance yet, but the layout has been designed for that future possibility.

Whilst the length and width of each station varied, by having a standard face at each end of the station any number of 'section' boards can be inserted to give an expandable run between stations. This also means that the layout size can vary depending on where it is set up. Whilst the polarity of the magnets joining the boards together means that they have to fit in one orientation, they do not necessarily have to be in the same place on the layout. Simple feeds to the track via male and female connector blocks eases the electrical issues whilst still allowing for a certain flexibility.

A baseboard width of 150mm was decided upon with the track centre either being 40mm from either edge or in the centre. Track height was set at 60mm allowing for some scenic potential below rail height. The layout is nominally flat.

By limiting the scenery above rail height, the maximum number of boards can stored in a box.

The corner boards have 355mm radius curves, so should it be desired even a continuous run could be arranged!

Using a number of extra tables, the home layout plan has been developed and can be adapted and expanded when space permits at other venues. A further station is under development allowing the system to expand.

So far we have not renamed the stations to fit in with the Andeer line, so our operators tend to call them by the prototype they were based on. They were not designed to be accurate models of the original but if people can see a similarity, that is fine by us.

Originally the design was a development of an 8' x 4' approach – actually 15'6" x 4'6". This required 'hiding' the dining table underneath the layout, hence the table top approach. The disadvantage of this particular plan was the 'dance' of operators around the edges of the layout and having 'control' in a different room! Also in many respects it was still along the theatre approach, with 'Pontresina' being the stage and the other two stations being the 'wings', albeit scenic. Lack of space dictated that 'Samedan' was always going to be more of a traditional fiddle yard!

Reconfiguring the baseboards and tables allowed a more traditional walk-around approach where the drivers actually move around the layout following their trains. This also allowed another station, based on Tirano, increasing the idea of going from A to B.

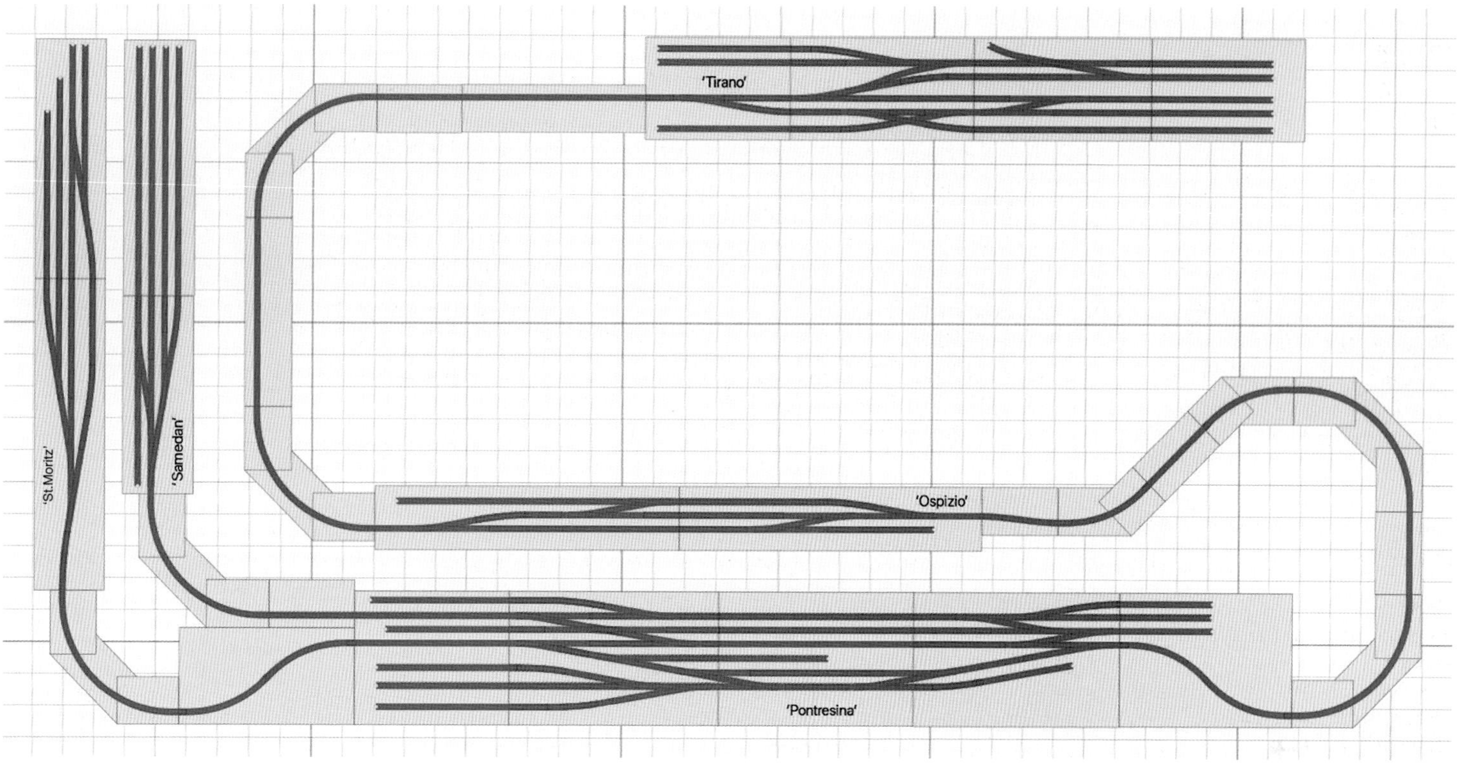

Above
The revised plan.

Below
Seeing trains run is always a source of encouragement. Being able to put part of the layout up is very useful for testing. It is also essential to make sure that the layout works before any scenery is begun. Note how the boards are supported on portable tables. Also note that this is not the eventual living room configuration – the ability to adapt is another advantage of modular design.

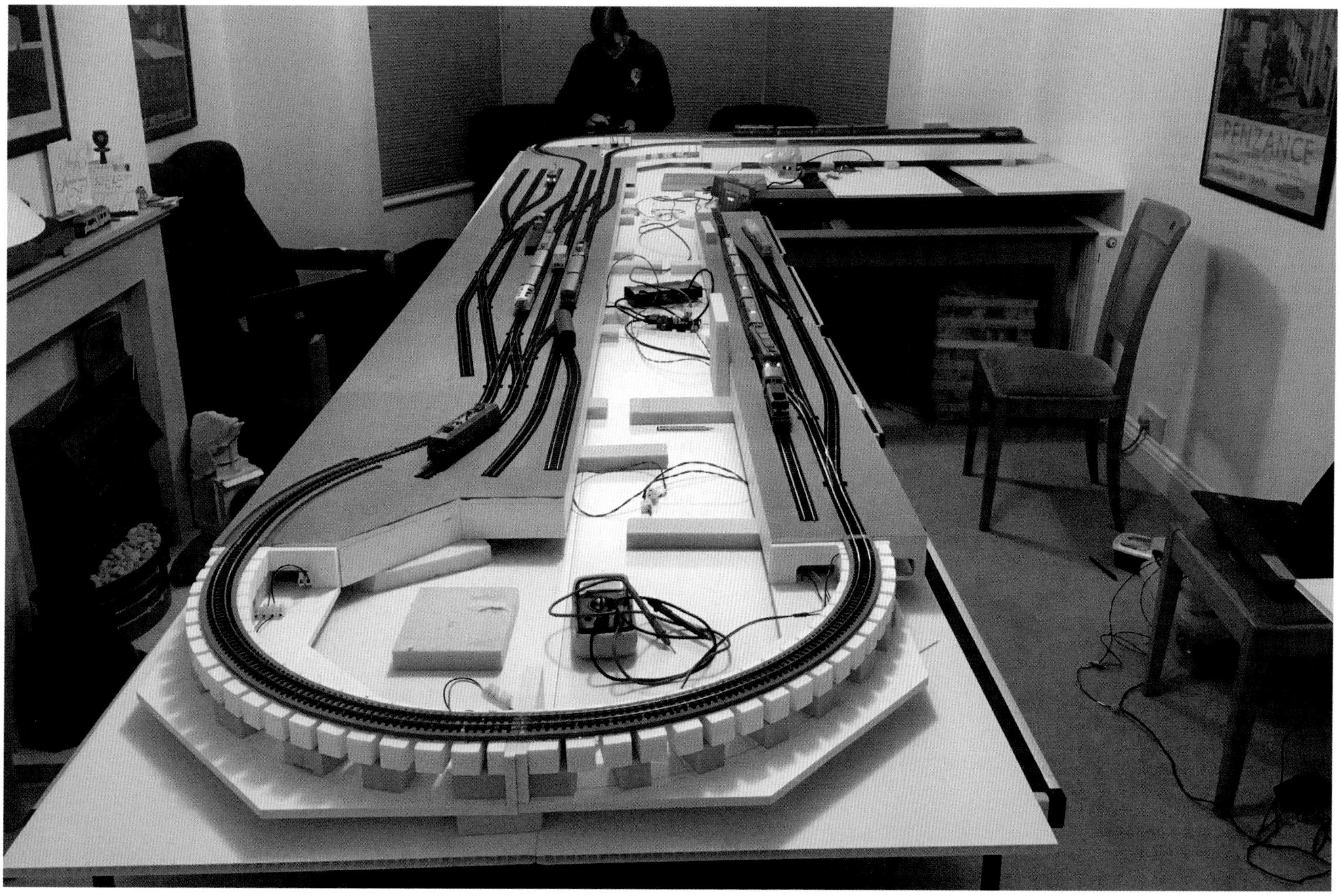

Left
Module components.

Right
A jig was constructed for making the end plates out of Foamalux. After careful measurement, the blanks for the end pieces were routed allowing consistent placement of magnets and dowels. Also in the picture are jigs for setting the depth of the router bit, an end awaiting completion, and the jigs for aligning the dowels within the boards.

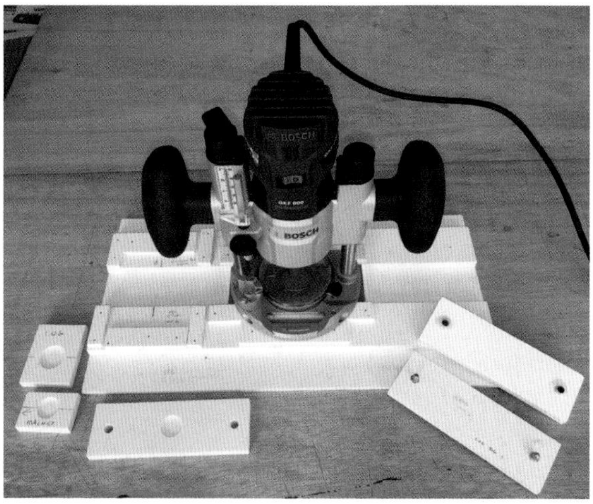

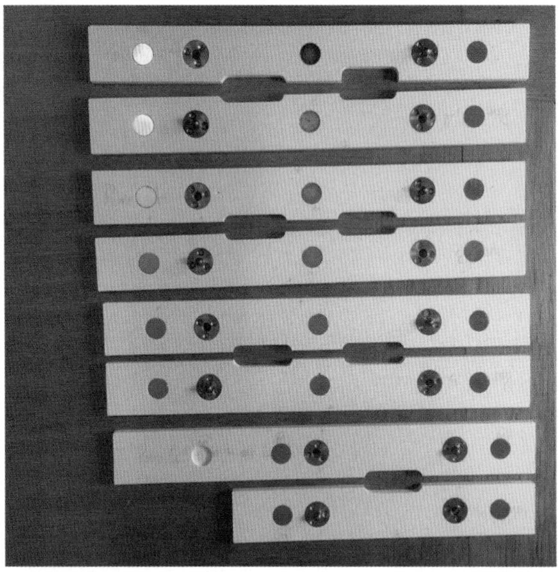

Left
These are the finished end plates for the Pontresina boards with the magnets, alignment dowels, and slots for wires. Due to the size of the DCC data link cables and the size of connector blocks, it was decided to stand the boards on strips of 25mm styrofoam to make connecting the baseboards and wires together easier. The additional weight in the storage box is negligible while keeping the baseboard depth to a minimum for optimum storage.

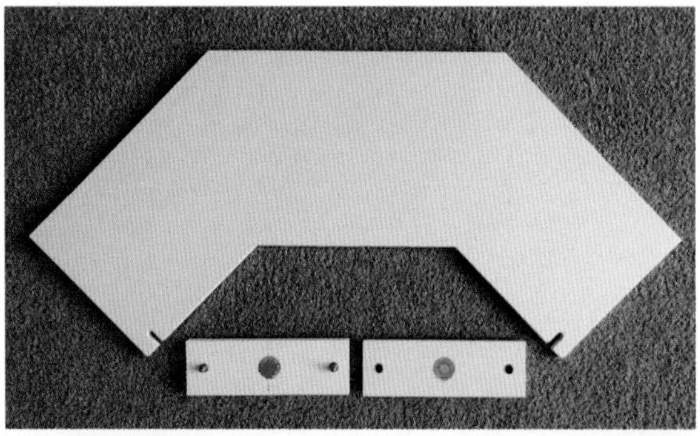

Left
Corner module parts.

Left
The intermediate boards were assembled using a hot glue gun on its highest setting – this allowed some adjustment before it set. Be careful with the excess glue!

The magnet can be useful for holding the end upright using a metal square.

The slots cut into the base allow the connector wires to be threaded neatly under the boards.

Construction

The baseboard foundations were made of 10mm foamboard. The larger stations are made using a traditional box method with a depth of 50mm to allow for point motors and control equipment.

The section boards between the stations are made using a solid base with the ends stuck on top forming a 'U' shape. A 5mm strip of white plastic provides a solid trackbed into which track pins can be inserted and the ends of the rails at the baseboard joints are soldered to copper-clad sleeper strip. The Foamalux tolerates a certain amount of heat transfer through the strip before it begins to melt! This also solved the problem of securing flexible track on the 90° curves. It also makes final alignment easier with the main baseboards when laying the track.

Once the design had been finalised, a jig for routing out dowel holes and magnet recesses was made. The ends are a simple rectangle with any scenery profile above track height at the baseboard end provided by Styrofoam – the scenery does not go below track level at the ends. Careful teamwork and a vacuum cleaner meant that the mess was minimal – all the routing was done in the flat. Usual precautions of ear defenders and safety glasses protected us and checking that the neighbours were out reduced any noise disturbance!

The Foamalux has been joined using either woodworking glue and screws or hot glue. The magnets have been secured by 'Gorilla Glue', care being taken to prevent the magnets being pushed out of the recess as the glue expands. Needless to say the polarity of the magnets was also checked carefully before insertion otherwise the baseboards would never join!

Below
The track was laid directly onto the Foamalux.

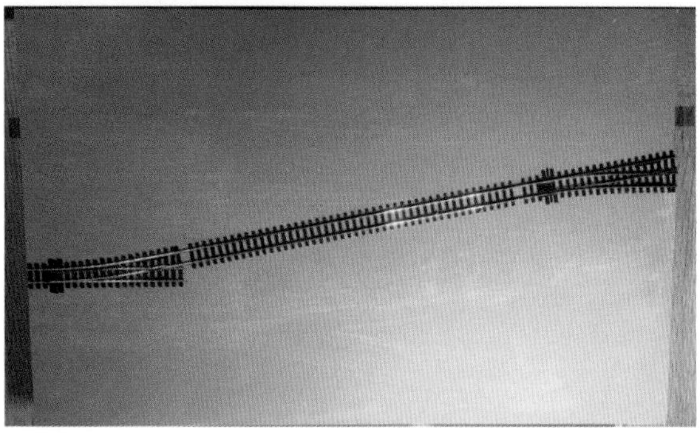

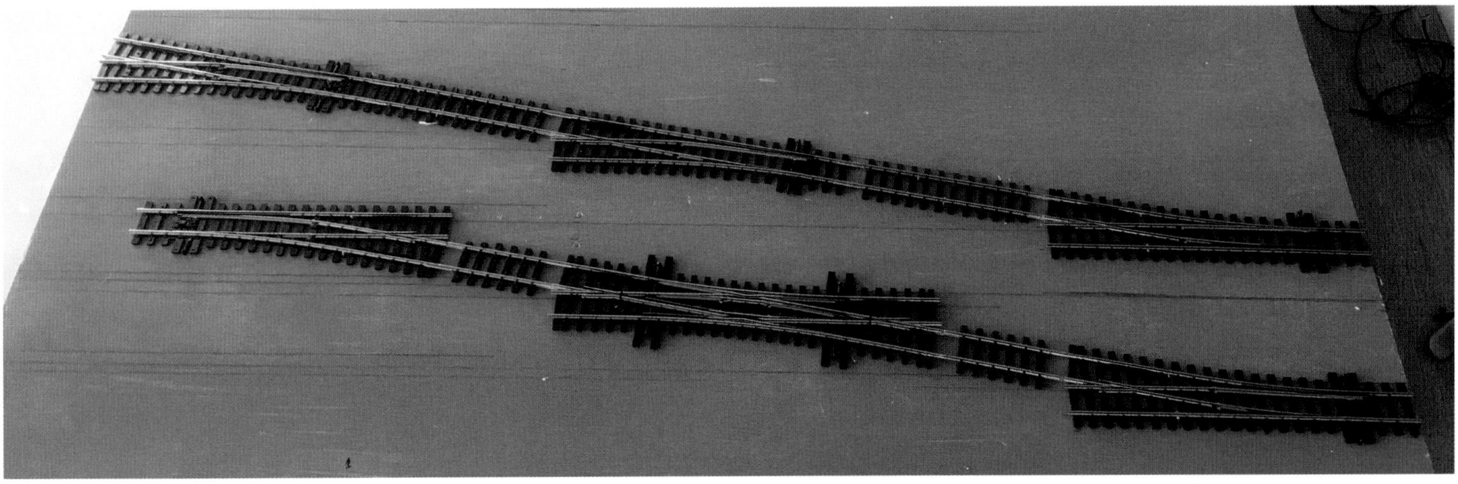

Above
The critical feature of the Pontresina design was the station throat at the St.Moritz end. This shows the formation laid out to check all was well. One side of the board (top left in this view) is shaped to match the diverging routes of the point. This non-standard join is matched by the next board and avoids the need for small pieces of track at the edges.

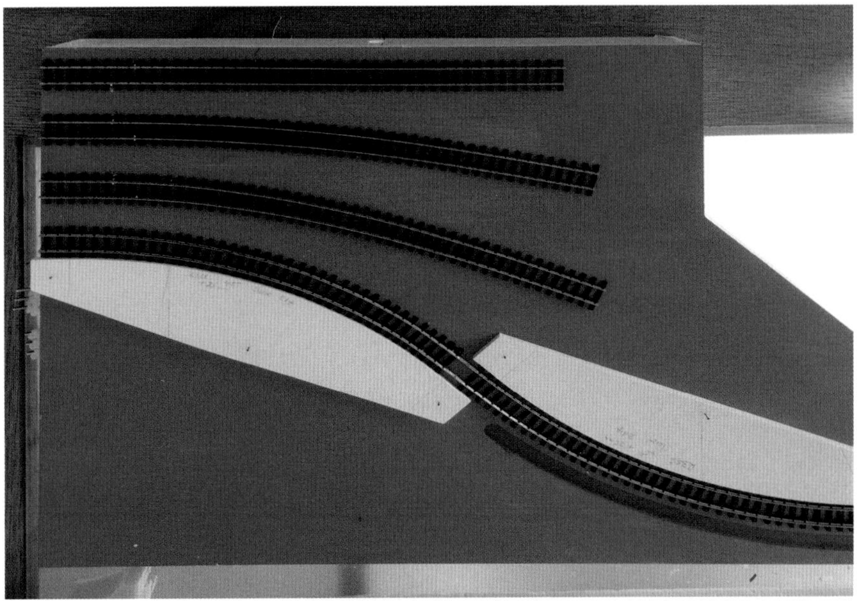

Right
The line to Tirano curves out of Pontresina and then onto a 'standard' 90° corner board. The curved track was laid using alignment jigs made from offcuts of 5mm Foamalux. A 20mm transition length was added 'by eye' (the mathematics being way too complicated!) – if it looks right, it is OK.

The track was laid directly on the Foamalux. In the station areas it was decided that there would not be that much of a ballast shoulder. On the scenic boards the 5mm thick strip was cut to 36mm wide which allows a ballast shoulder. The ballast has been laid using dilute wood glue or scenic cement, whichever was to hand.

Left
The track laid, with stock in place for inspiration. These are the two centre boards for Pontresina, looking towards Tirano. The line to Samedan is second from the left at the board join in the bottom of the picture, that to St.Moritz fourth from the left. The three tracks on the right serve the stock storage shed.

Right
The two centre boards for Pontresina seen from the other end, looking towards St.Moritz and Samedan. When set up for operation, Pontresina is the other way round within the living room.

Above
Tall mountain scenery was not high on our list of priorities. To maximise the use of the storage capacity, many items are removable, such as trees and taller buildings. The trees are fitted into tubes to reduce the wear and tear on the foam scenery. Because of the wiring, signals are left in place; collars made from plastic cups serve as a reminder of their presence though not complete protection.

Scenery

Our priorities and restrictions also mean that we are never going to be able to recreate the mountain grandeur of Switzerland as seen on many other layouts. For higher background scenery, separate sections can be added, if necessary held in place by magnets located on the side of the main boards.

The basis for the scenery was Styrofoam recycled from the previous layout filled and painted with emulsion paint. This was then covered with various products from the Peco Scene and Woodland Scenics ranges. The trees, mostly simple affairs from K&M, are 'planted' in a brass tube so they can be removed to reduce storage space requirements. This does mean that the scenery may vary each time the layout is put together.

Although the width of the boards does not allow for much scenery, when driving most of the attention is on the train and its immediate surroundings, and just as in real life the driver should be concentrating on the track and signals ahead and not gazing at the (non-existent) scenery!

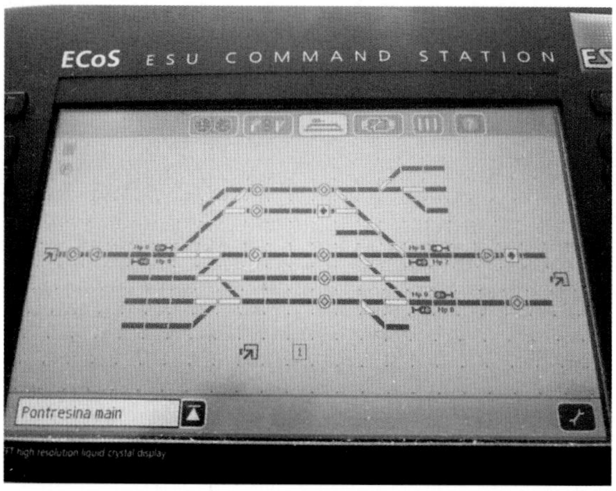

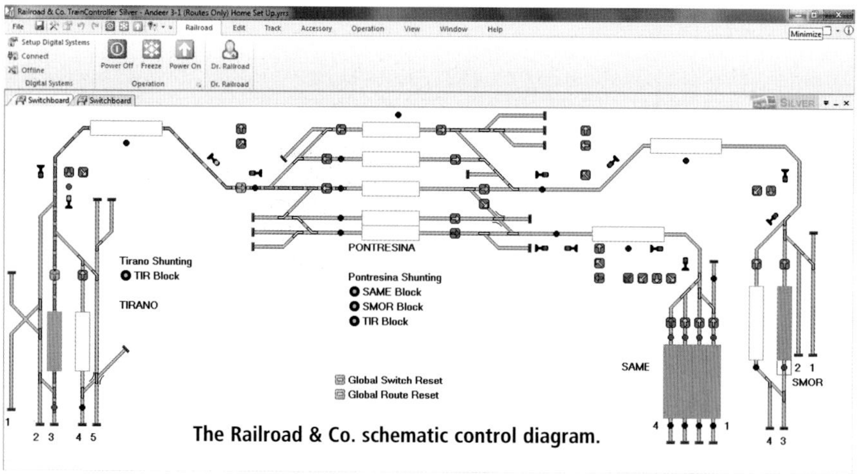

The Railroad & Co. schematic control diagram.

Control

The basis of control is by DCC, from an ESU ECoS system. There are those who say digital is just two wires to the track: that is the theory and the basic practice, but once things such as point motors, working signals, and track detection are taken into consideration the number of wires increases rapidly! However, from our experience, fault finding is logical and much simpler than with DC. Planning for the electrical systems was something that was taken into consideration in the design stage and has worked out reasonably well.

All the running lines are detected with a fully working signalling system based on RhB practice. The touch screen of the ECoS allows a simple central signal box to be set up very quickly to control the whole layout (*below left*). Route setting is done by the 'entry – exit' principle which sets points and signals as required. The detection is used to return the signals to red automatically after the passage of a train.

A mixture of iPhones and iPads using the 'TouchCab' app and a wi-fi router are used to allow drivers to follow their trains around the layout. Similar apps are available for Android devices and guest operators bring their own devices, making this an easy and inexpensive way of increasing the number of operators. Any smart 'phone with a suitable app can be used.

At exhibitions visitors are often invited to drive, and it may be a sign of the times that using these devices the younger generation pick up the technique particularly quickly.

One of the disadvantages of having the central signal box on the ECoS system is the inability to see the whole layout on one screen. To overcome this we have introduced a PC running Railroad & Co. software (*above*). This also allows a degree of train automation, should we require it. As the social side of the hobby is one of the most important, in our opinion, having human drivers is much more appealing. When the PC is in use, the ECoS unit is used to control Pontresina allowing the station supervisor to operate points locally, and drive the shunting loco as well. A series of 'software locks' prevents conflicting routes being set. However, this does not stop inattentive drivers passing signals at danger – though fortunately without the serious consequences of the real thing.

We try to run to a sequence based a typical day's passenger and freight movements over the Bernina line. Whatever system is used to control the layout, communication between station supervisors, drivers, and central control is essential. The human interaction between operators is all part of the fun and points can be amassed for good and bad operations with an award at the end of the day for best / worst operator. All done with good humour!

Conclusion

As with most layouts, *The Andeer line* is a work in progress. Being modular there is the possibility of expansion by building more scenic boards or stations. It has been set up and operated a number of times in different locations. The basic principle has been shown to be sound, and the dream has become a reality. It is an attempt to combine the experiences of operating a railway system, not just one station, within the constraints imposed by personal circumstances. Its style might not be to everyone's taste but it is enjoyable to operate, and the design and development process is a continuing rewarding challenge. Meeting people with a variety of interests and experience has been a superb way to develop and improve skills. Great friendships have been forged extending outside the hobby. Railway modelling has many sides to it which is one of its big attractions and what should always be remembered is that it is supposed to be fun!

PENZANCE
GREAT WESTERN RAILWAY
CORNWALL
SOUTHERN RAILWAY

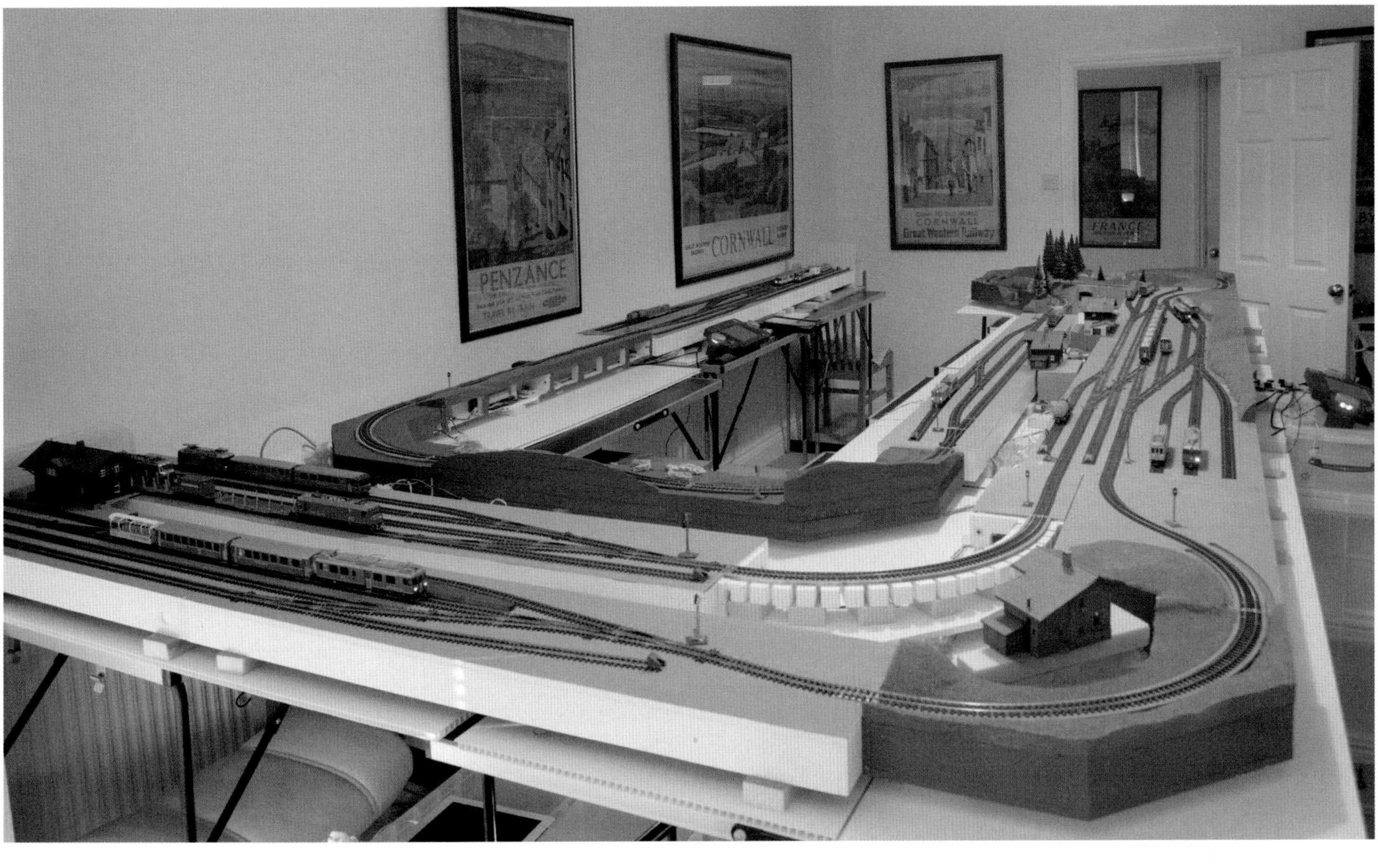
PENZANCE
CORNWALL
CORNWALL
Great Western Railway
FRANCE

Country halt

Peter Marriott builds a laser-cut card kit for a small rural station building in HO.
Photographs by the author.

Laser-cut card is one of the newer materials now available to modellers and is used for buildings, fencing, bridges, windows, doors, and even plants and vegetables. The latest releases demonstrate that laser-cut card and wood can be delicate but also very strong.

Aku, Busch, Joswood, Faller, Fides, Laser Creation, Noch and Tip Top Modell are just some of the companies producing laser-cut card kits of buildings suitable for Swiss layouts. The Busch and Noch ranges include small buildings such as garden sheds and kiosks.

The subject of this feature is one of the smaller ones from Faller, with parts made from card, thin wood, plastic, paper, and clear plastic (for the windows).

I found the mainly pictorial instructions to be very good.

The laser-cut card and wood parts are held on backing sheets by small tabs that must be carefully cut through before assembly can begin. I found that the parts were very cleanly cut, which made assembly very easy.

Use a steel ruler and a cutting board when cutting laser cut materials. This applies even if you are only cutting through the small tabs to separate the pieces from the backing card. The steel ruler directs the cutting strokes more positively and the cutting board protects the surface below.

Only use new blades when working with laser-cut materials because blades that are tired may leave torn edges and require more cutting strokes.

UHU *Holz Leim* or Busch *Laser Cut Kleber* are useful adhesives that give a short drying time when assembling laser-cut kits. These glues are available from Gaugemaster and Golden Valley Hobbies and other retailers.

If you get excess glue onto the surface as it is being assembled, remove it with a damp cloth as quickly as possible – if the adhesive is left to dry, it will result in a shiny mark on the finished model.

Felt tip pens, weathering dyes, or a thin wash of acrylic paint can be used to colour and hide any exposed corners and joints of the laser-cut materials once the kit is assembled.

Building the kit is in two stages: firstly the inner walls are assembled, then the laser-cut wood pieces are overlaid.

After the windows have been added to the building, the curtains are added by folding the paper insert and pushing it inside the structure.

Next the guttering, downpipes, shutters, and barge boards can be added.

After I had finished the kit, I added a fictional station sign in the correct SBB font made on my computer.

It took about two hours to make this kit in total, excluding the drying time of the adhesives and paint.

This would be very good for a modeller new to laser-cut kits as it easy to assemble and looks very realistic.

Tools and materials

- Sharp craft knife
- Steel ruler
- Self-sealing cutting board
- Small paint brushes to paint cut edges
- Acrylic paints to paint cut card and wood edges
- Felt tip pens for touching up card edges
- Small pair of tweezers to position small details
- Adhesive

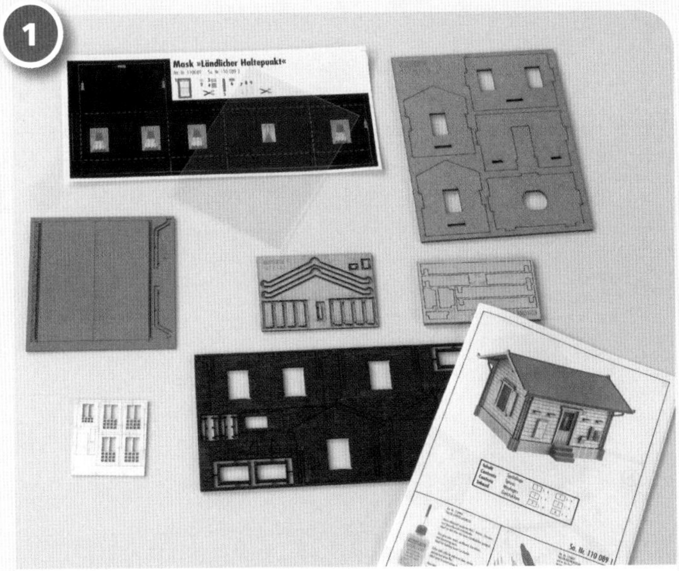

The parts are made from card, thin wood, plastic, paper, and clear plastic (for the windows).

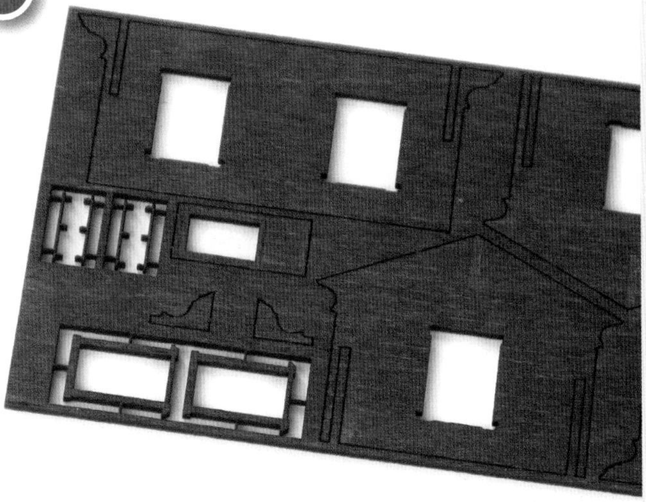

One of the wooden walls showing the small tabs that hold the pieces in place which must be removed before assembly.

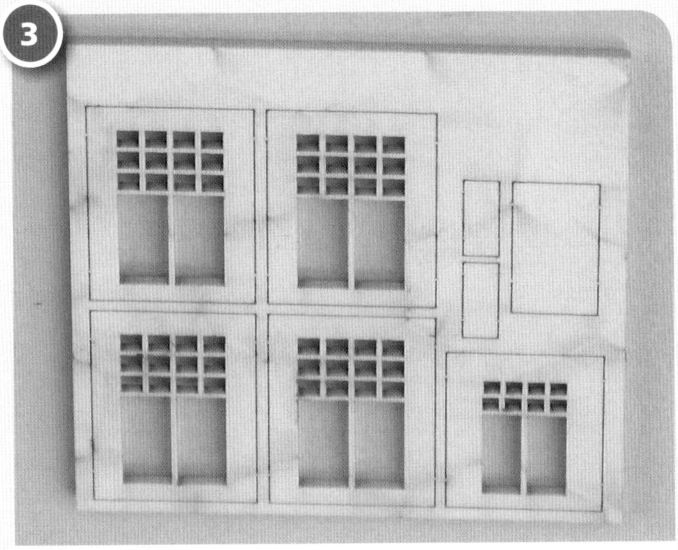

The window pieces are very cleanly cut out.

Basic assembly of the kit.

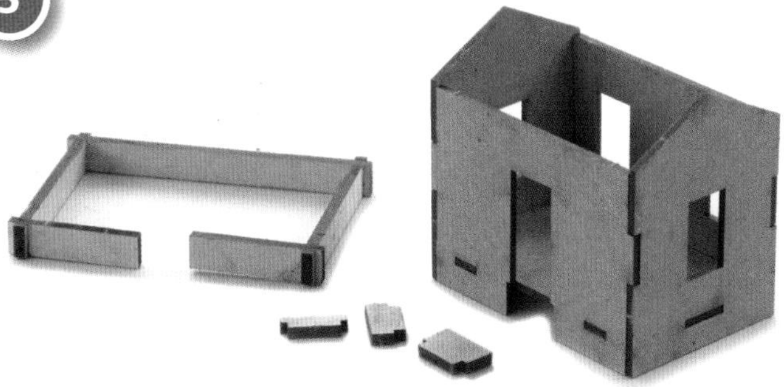

The four walls and floor have been assembled and we are now working on the lower part of the building.

A window frame, the steps, and a roof support bracket after being removed from the main backing pieces.

7

The basic frame for the building has been made and the steps are being added.

8

The laser-cut wood overlay parts ready to clad the basic frame.

9

Adhesive has been spread onto the end wall of the building before the overlay is added.

10

The delicate wood window frames being installed – the right hand one is in, the left hand is to be done.

11

After the windows have been fitted, the curtains need to be added inside. The supplied paper insert must be folded and then pushed inside the building.

12

After the roof is added, the gutters, down pipes, and barge boards can be fitted.

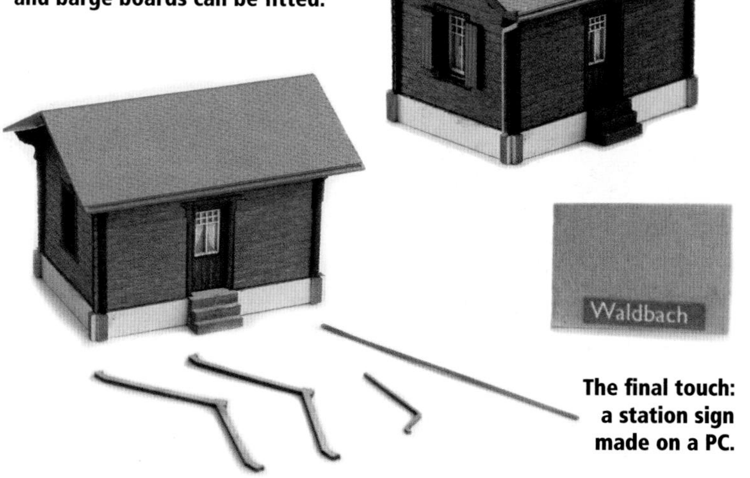

The final touch: a station sign made on a PC.

Fahrplan
Waldbach

Fahrplan
Waldbach

Waldbach

Below
Diesel locomotive HGm4/4 62 built in 1968 by SLM, BBC and MFO with a Cummins engine hauls Breda-built panoramic coaches from the As 4021–30 series away from Gletsch station up towards the summit tunnel. Although this part had to be shortened in the model, features such as the wooden retaining walls have been faithfully reproduced.

A metre gauge rack railway in an impressive mountain landscape

Gletsch

Willi Rutz has accurately recreated in HOm the summit station at Gletsch and a section of the Furka Oberalp line towards Oberwald.

The Furka Bergstecke, or mountain line, could only be used in the summer and was replaced after 1981 by a base tunnel which allowed year-round operation. The last steam train ran over the mountain pass line in October 1981 and the new tunnel opened in June 1982.

Background

In 1959, while I was still at school, I travelled with my parents in the family VW 'Beetle' over the Furka and Grimsel passes. Later, during my apprenticeship as a mechanical engineer (1968) I was able to ride the railway over the Furka Pass. I had also ridden my racing bike several times over the Furka and nearby passes. But it was not until the mountain section of the railway, from Oberwald to Realp, was closed and replaced by the base tunnel, that I really got interested in the Furka Oberalp as a subject to model.

I was increasingly drawn to Gletsch station, high in the mountains, 1,759m above sea level. The track layout offered more than the usual passing station, with freight sidings, a cattle dock, a loco shed, and even a turntable. Another distinctive feature was that the station building was on the other side of the river, reached by a bridge. Also, the whole site was not too large – I thought it should be possible to reproduce it to scale in 1:87. (Previous modelling projects had foundered because the choice of prototype had proved too large to do this.) I also wanted to do something a bit different, and I had not seen many layouts reproducing the rack sections.

I had been collecting both Rhätische Bahn and Furka Oberalp models in HOm, with items from specialists as well as the mainstream Bemo. I reckoned that if those expensive hand-crafted models were so accurate, the layout had to be to the same standard.

I could not obtain a proper track plan, either from the railway or the society which had then recently been formed to save the mountain line. So in the autumn of 1983, having prepared rough drawings, I went to Gletsch equipped with camera, notepad, measuring tape, and spirit level and made a detailed record of the station site and surrounding landscape. This was necessary not only for the station but also the surroundings to be represented exactly as there was no other source of information.

(I stayed for three nights in a 'rustic' room in the large Glacier du Rhône hotel near the station – unforgettable!)

Between 1985 and 1987 I worked on modelling the station in 1:87. Two years intensive work produced the substructure, the track, and the shell of the scenery. However, the demands of work (often abroad) then took precedence and the dream had to be put aside – until 2001. Then I had access to a large hobby room, and the project could not only be continued but extended towards Oberwald to the portal of the spiral tunnel.

Above
**A short shuttle train leaves the upper storage yard through the tunnel at the highest point of the layout.
The small three-arch stone bridge is an authentic feature.**

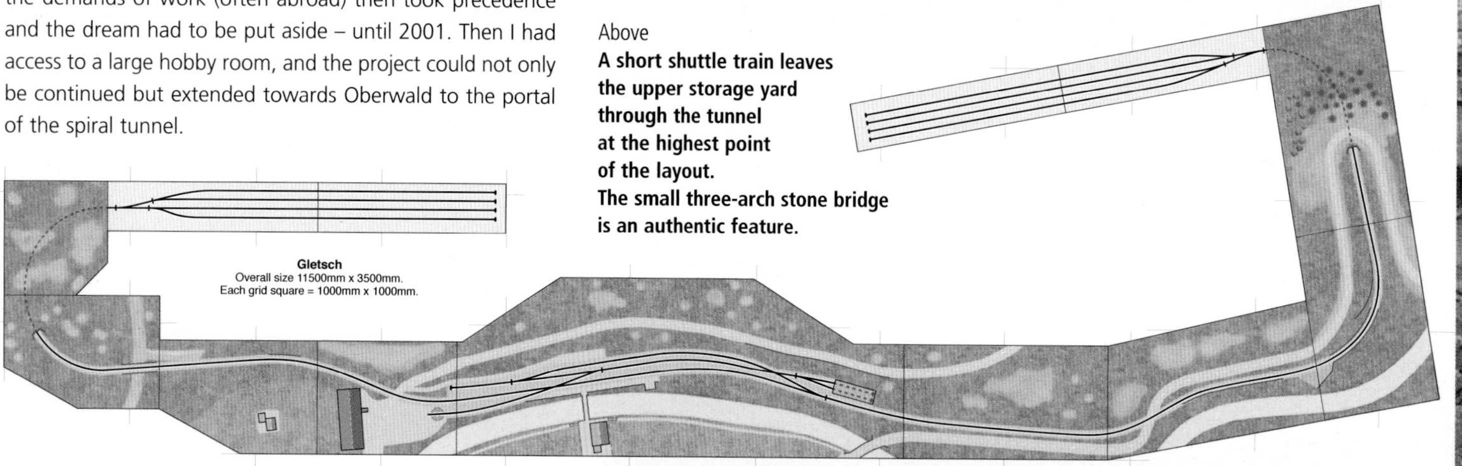

Furka-Oberalp

Above
HGe4/4I 34 climbs the gradient with a train for Andermatt. The farm building accommodates the local shepherd.

The resulting layout is on ten separate baseboards arranged in a long L shape, 11.5m long and 3.5m wide. There are five further boards, for the two storage yards behind the layout and the Furka mountain road.

The climb from the lowest point to the highest is about 80cm.

The layout

The layout shown here is set in the period 1965 to 1980, and represents the section around Gletsch station modelled exactly to scale.

The upper section, leaving the storage sidings through the portal of the summit tunnel, drops through curves towards Gletsch station. The landscape is rather barren above the tree line. This part is not to scale length but includes characteristic features. After crossing a small curved bridge, the line reaches the station.

Near the level crossing, which is equipped with working warning lights, is the large Hotel Glacier du Rhône, also known as the 'Blue House'. Several railway enthusiasts with cameras can be seen round the crossing.

Gletsch station offers not only the opportunity to cross trains but also various freight facilities. The cattle dock is an important feature; cattle transport plays a significant rôle and wagons are often seen here.

There is also a two road loco shed, with sloped roof to deflect rockfalls, where steam locos can be stored and have their supplies replenished – the necessary installations are naturally represented on the model.

At the other end of the station there is a turntable, which was primarily used for turning snow ploughs and snow blowers although also used by locomotives, as some services terminated or originated here.

The other unusual feature of the site is that, due to lack of space on the side of the mountain, the station building is on the other side of the river, reached by a metal footbridge. Tall natural stone walls protect the station yard and building from flooding when the melt water swells the river.

The line drops from the station and weaves its way over a bridge designed to withstand avalanches down to the entrance of the spiral tunnel.

The mountain road is close to the line here. The road vehicles are correct for the period.

At each end of the layout there are storage yards.

The track in the station was built from Ferro-Suisse kits, while the steep rack sections and the track in the hidden areas is Bemo (Shinohara).

The catenary is by Sommerfeldt, with some scratchbuilt elements.

All types of motive power can be used on the layout.

All the locos and railcars are by Bemo, fitted with Zimo DCC decoders. Control is by wireless handsets. Points are operated by toggle switches on the control panel.

Other products used include STL, Fulgurex, Motreno, and Hapo.

Top
HG3/4 2-6-0T No.10 waits with two old four-wheel coaches. On the other siding, small snowplough X4903 is stabled with a coach converted for overhead line maintenance.

Above
The shuttle train passes the 'Blue House', the Glacier du Rhône Hotel, where the staff of the Furka mountain steam railway are accommodated now. At this period, the mountain road still had a gravel surface.

Below

During the summer season Gletsch could be very busy. A regional train pulls in to pass the *Glacier Express* and the museum steam train waits on the siding. The turntable was necessary for turning snow ploughs and blowers as well as locomotives.

Below
By the station building a small music group (singers, accordions, and barrel organ) greet travellers.

Buildings

The fully accurate depiction of the station is due to the complete scratchbuilding of all the buildings, with some commercial components used where possible.

Not only has everything been reproduced precisely to size but also realistically coloured and weathered.

The Hotel Glacier du Rhône is said to have gained the nickname 'The Blue House' because in earlier times the end of the glacier was much further down the valley and the building looked blue in the reflected light of the full moon.

Landscape and vegetation

Just as the buildings are meticulously modelled, the landscape is also exactly like the real thing.

Bushes interrupt scree and rock areas.

As far as there are any trees at this high altitude, they have been scratchbuilt.

Not to be forgotten is the skillful representation of the water, showing the relatively light summer flow of the river, which represents the young Rhône, here known as the Rotter.

Below
**Here the line runs alongside the mountain road from Gletsch to the Furka pass. The road was surveyed accurately specifically for the project so the landscape would be genuine.
In the gorge flows a realistically modelled river, the Rotter, which will become the Rhône.**

Photographs by the editor.

Cameo scenes

Above the portal of the summit tunnel, a group of clearly experienced walkers are taking a short pause before continuing.

In another place a hunter with raised rifle is preparing to shoot a bear.

The young Rhône is clearly rich in fish. On a gravel bank in the centre, downstream of the station, two fly-fishermen are swinging their rods. Will they catch trout or perhaps something else?

But even that is not enough movement: the cows move their heads and swing their tails.

Meanwhile a stork circles over a courting couple in the bushes; they are oblivious to the fact they can be seen.

Above the cattle loading scene a Rapid rider with empty milk churns seems to be in a hurry.

A Setra tour bus significantly reduces its speed as it comes down the pass road towards the level crossing – which is often closed due to trains passing.

Outside the station a local choir is performing, accompanied by two accordions and a barrel organ. The music comes from a concealed sound module.

The figures are by Preiser and Viessmann.

Future prospects

I wanted to continue building the line beyond the spiral tunnel, and to mount the whole layout one metre higher, because at the moment the lower end is nearly on the floor. Unfortunately, due to moving house, I lost the large hobby room and in my current dwelling I can only set up the three station boards. The other boards are stored in the garage. I cannot find a larger hobby room to rent at a reasonable rate so that I can enjoy the whole layout. This is now only possible at exhibitions.

The layout has made around thirty exhibition appearances, being set up in its entirety for the first time at the Frauenfeld *Trains and Trucks* exhibition in 2008. Later events included the Specialist Suppliers show in Bauma (Switzerland), Intermodellbau in Dortmund in 2014, and the IMA in Köln in November 2016.

Since January 2017, there has been a change of plan: the layout is being permanently installed in the Good Night Inn hotel in Brig. It is being converted from point-to-point operation to a continuous run with automatic operation, with more scenic sections in place of the storage yards. It is not yet open to the public.

Above
A shuttle train travels down towards the entrance of the tunnel (and the lower storage sidings) and passes over an emergency bridge, constructed as a result of avalanche damage.

Below
A Deh 4/4 motor luggage van heading for Gletsch with a short train.
From here to the upper tunnel the difference in height is almost a metre!

Making authentic details

Posters and signs

Peter Marriott shows how to create signs from your own photos and printed material.
Photographs by the author.

Adding signs and station posters is one of the little details that does not take a lot of time or cost a lot but really can make a big visual difference, helping to determine the layout's location or intended time period. Signs and posters may be on and around the station, on station buildings, or platforms, or railway land. In addition there are trackside railway signs, street signs, shop signs, industrial company signs, advertising hoardings, road signs, and footpath signs.

Various manufacturers produce signs and posters for Swiss situations, including Microscale, Aubertrain, and Modellbau Atelier. Kibri print signs on the boxes of their plastic kits, and the Noch laser-cut range includes a number of track signs. There is also an excellent choice of free to download signs at the Viessmann/Kibri website

http://www.viessmann-modell.com/index.php
show=categories&cPath=110_129&cId=129&lang=de

Alternatively it can be fun to make your own signs by taking digital pictures then working with them on a computer to bring them to scale and then printing them in colour.

When you are researching your chosen location, take 'square on' pictures of the signs that you might want to reproduce in miniature. Take several pictures of the same sign using different zoom settings and chose which image is closest to the scale you are working in when you see it on screen.

In my experience, home-made signs take about twenty minutes each to make. By comparison, it takes just about five minutes to install a purchased sign.

Some signs come on cardboard and must be carefully cut round with a sharp craft knife and steel ruler. The white edges of the sign can be 'painted' by carefully running a black marker pen around them. Never leave the cut edges of card uncoloured. It takes just one minute per sign to colour the edges.

Cut a length of plastic rod and fix to the reverse of the sign with contact adhesive or superglue. Paint the reverse of the sign and the post with acrylic paints.

Do not get carried away and overdo the use of signs. Layouts that feature too many look cluttered and unrealistic.

Sources

www.mbapiro.ch
www.microscale.ch
www.aubertrain.com

Above left
A 'Kagi' advertising poster which I wanted to use.

Above
A large poster promoting Kandersteg seen at Frutigen. Always take pictures of signs you might want 'square on'.

Tools and materials

- Craft knife with spare blades
- Steel ruler
- Self-sealing cutting board
- Black felt tip marker pen to colour the edges of the cut card.
- Selection of paint brushes, including micro-brushes
- Pin vice with suitable bit for drilling holes to take the posts
- Thin cardboard to back the homemade printed paper signs
- Fine plastic rod (such as Evergreen) to form the posts
- Primer for painting bare metal posts
- Matt acrylic paint grey to paint the posts and the backs of the signs
- A glue stick or white glue to fix the sign or poster to the cardboard

Station platform poster board

1

The photograph of the Kandersteg poster was printed in several sizes until I got the correct scale size for HO. On the left, the poster has been fixed to a piece of thin card.

2

A selection of other posters photographed at Swiss stations.

3

The Kandersteg poster and one of the classic Lötschbergbahn signs from Kandersteg station ready to be installed.

4

Microscale produce station advertisements with a selection of posters, in packs of two boards and a sheet of posters (ref. 201).

5

A Kagi advertising poster, on the platform at Neuchâtel.

6

Once I had copied the file from camera to computer, I printed the poster in various sizes to see which was best for HO.

7

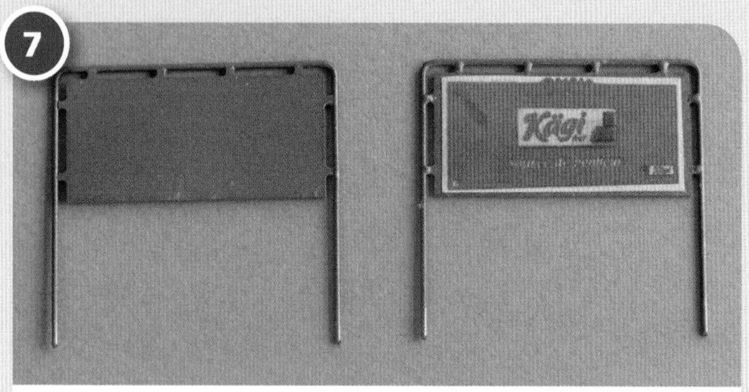

I then fixed the printed Kagi poster to one of the Microscale poster boards using a glue stick. These metal poster boards usefully come ready primed and painted.

8

A Swiss postman by Noch next to the poster board.

9

The Kagi poster fixed to the Microscale poster board. Two small holes were drilled into the platform to take the posts.

10

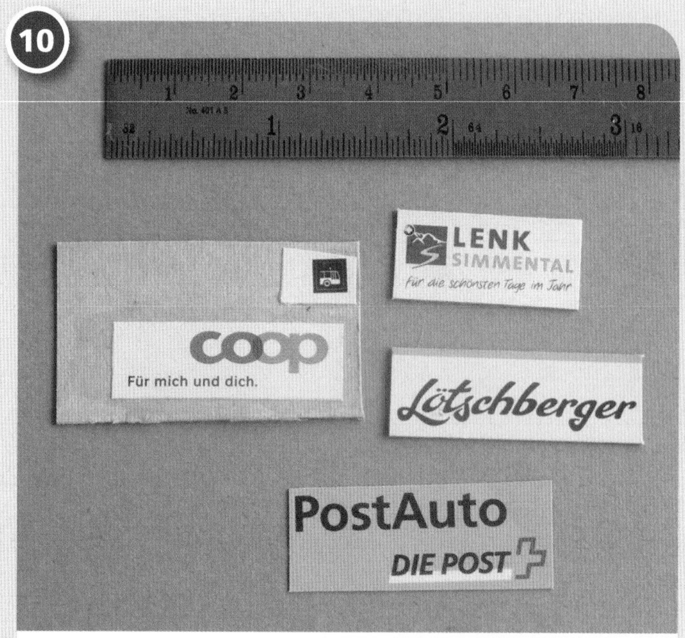

A selection of small signs cut from various advertising leaflets – another good source of material – fixed to thin card.

11

After two hours work I had a station sign with a poster made from one of my own pictures and a selection of signs collected from a variety of Swiss sources – including a packet of biscuits!

'Do not cross the track' sign

1

One of the most common signs at Swiss stations is the 'Do not cross the lines' notice between the tracks, in four languages.

2

A slight variation – a 'Do not cross the lines' sign with the posts set into concrete bases.

3

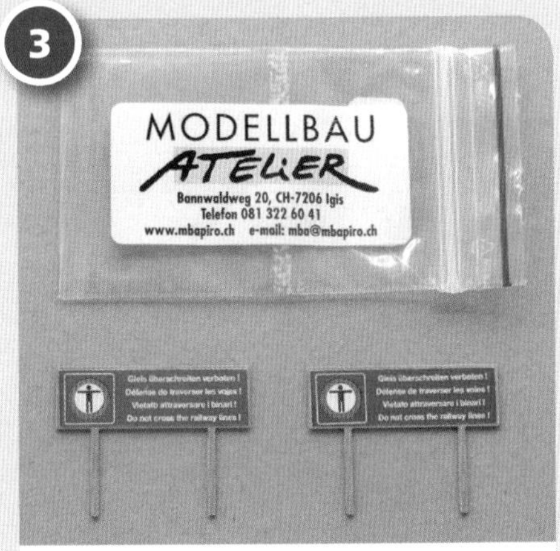

In HO 'Do not cross the railway lines' signs are available in packs of two ready to use from Modellbau Atelier.

4

The 'Do not cross the railway lines' signs can also be made from your own photographs of actual signs printed on good quality photo paper, mounted on card, with plastic rod for the posts.

5

A home-made 'Do not cross the lines' sign in place on the layout.

Footpath signs

Switzerland has one of the best marked footpath networks in the world and adjacent to most railway stations there are various footpath signs. This one is at Reichenbach im Kandertal.

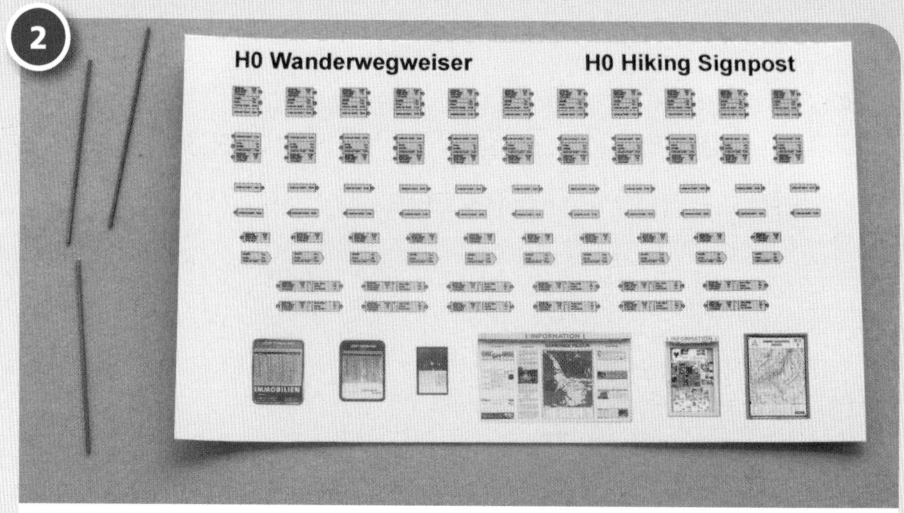

Modellbau Atelier produce a pack with a sheet of footpath and Post bus signs with eight metal posts which should be primed and painted before the signs are attached.

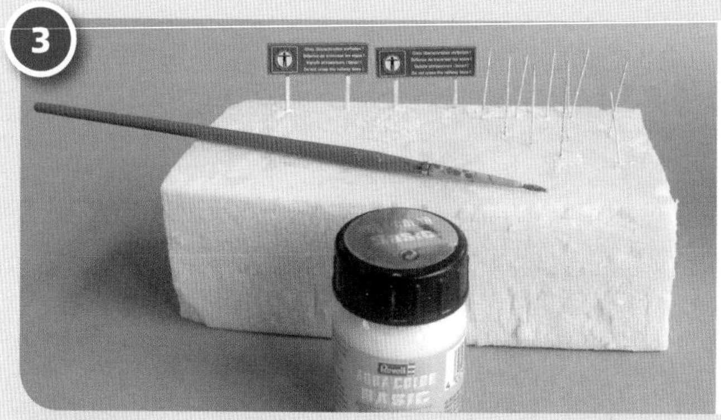

In real life, most of the posts of the footpath signs are light grey.
After the primer has dried, paint the posts using an acrylic paint.

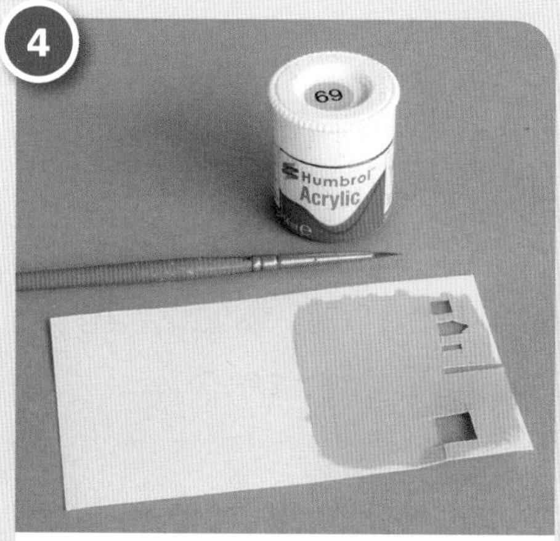

Before I cut out any of the signs, I painted the back of the sheet yellow using Humbrol acrylic 69. This may seem a small thing but if the reverse side is left white it will be obvious.

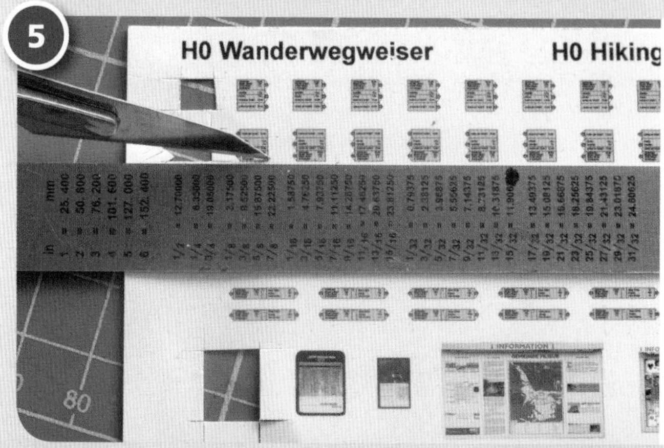

To cut the signs off the sheet, I put a new blade in my craft knife and used a steel ruler over a self-sealing cutting board. Working carefully will be rewarded. Even so, it took just an hour to assemble four signs, including a Post bus timetable.

Four signs, including the Post bus timetable, ready to be placed.

Two signs on the layout.

A small slice of Switzerland in N

A loft layout

Peter Marriott introduces the developing N gauge layout of David Aldis. *Photographs by the author.*

Over the past few years I have been assisting David Aldis with the scenery on the N scale layout in his loft. When I began work on the project in 2011 David had laid most of the track on plain timber. The challenge he set me was to turn the timber into something that looked a lot more like Switzerland.

Both David and I visit Switzerland as often as we can and he had long list of requirements for his layout, including double track main lines diving in and out of trees, cut grass alongside the track, rock faces, a passing loop station, a cable car, a road crossing the tracks, and much more.

The layout is vaguely based on the BLS (with its model of the Bietschtal Viaduct) but rolling stock is used that would be seen throughout the country – basically whatever takes his fancy.

The layout is located in the loft and measures approximately 18' x 10', with the baseboards about 2' wide arranged around the four sides of the space. Half of the layout has scenery with the remainder being used for storage sidings. There are two main levels with double track lines on both, plus a branch line leading up to a third level. The track was weathered with various shades of track dirt or sleeper grime mainly using Railmatch aerosols.

Landscape foundations are a mixture of timber, hard foam, plaster cloth, and cork bark. The scenic materials are mainly Woodland Scenics 'Fine Turf' and 'Poly Fiber', static grass fibres by Noch, and Greenscene light grey tarmac textured paint. Adhesives are mainly PVA and extra hold hairspray.

Above
BLS Stadler GTW unit (Piko).

Above right
The station building is a plastic kit bought cheaply.

Below
The station has a double track main line, two loops, and a short siding, currently holding a BLS Robel Tm235 unit (Hobbytrain).
The double-deck stock is by Fleischmann and the Re460 locomotives by Kato.

So far there are over three hundred trees on the layout, with at least another two hundred to be planted.

The buildings are a mixture of Faller, Vollmer, and Pola, with figures by Noch. The road vehicles, including a number of obligatory Post buses, are by Rietze, Wiking, and Faller.

The locomotives and rolling stock are by (in alphabetical order) Arnold, Brawa, Creanorm, Eriam, Fleischmann, Fulgurex, Hag, Hobbytrain, Hochstrasse, Ibertren, Kato, Lemaco, Liliput, Lima Minitrain, Mehano, Minitrix, Piko, Roco, and Wabu. It is quite a collection.

The accompanying pictures represent four years work. I could only get to work on the layout for a few hours about three times a year as we live about 200 miles apart and generally each time I visited the boot of my car was full of plaster cloth, hard foam, paint aerosols, poly fibre, rock pieces, and scatter materials. Part of the purpose of my visits was to show David what to do. He picked up the skills very quickly and was a most enthusiastic student.

The area around the Bietschtal Viaduct is still to be completed, along with the installation of catenary and some signals. That will take at least another two years to complete.

It has been fun to work with David on this layout.

Right
SBB Cargo 'Re10/10' passes the main station. The locomotives are Re6/6 620 058 (Kato) and Re4/4 421 397 (Fleischmann).

Right
All three levels of track are visible in this picture. The top level is single track, the middle and lower levels are double track. SBB 'Red Arrow' railcar (Hobbytrain) on the top level and SBB Ae6/6 11443 (Fleischmann) on the middle level.

Below
The *Trans Europ Express* RABDe 8/12 is a Kato model.

Scenic construction

1

How the three levels of the layout appeared seven years ago. The main lines were on timber supports with additional hard foam pieces on top of the timber.

2

Various rock pieces were made using Woodland Scenics moulds and then coloured with Woodland Scenics 'Earth Colours'.

3

As an experiment, pieces of the rock were positioned between the track levels to see how the finished layout might look.

4

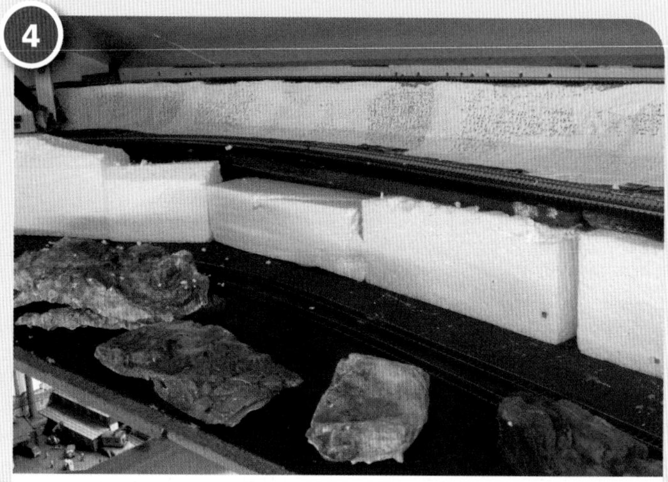

Between the higher two levels of track plaster cloth has been draped between the track supports. Between the lower two levels hard foam pieces have been positioned ready to shape.

5

Rock pieces were positioned on the steep slopes between the track and blended with the landscape using modelling compound from Busch and Noch.

6

The track was covered with card while green acrylic paint from an aerosol coloured the areas that would be covered in grass. The rocks were painted with a first layer of grey paint.

7

Between the rock faces Woodland Scenics 'Poly Fiber' was teased out and glued in position to represent lineside vegetation and bushes. The scenery to the left of the line is on its own sub-base as it was developed separately.

8

A piece of untreated cork bark which will be used to represent other rock faces on the layout. Lots of pieces of this material had been collected over ten years before building the layout.

9

Cork bark pieces positioned between the lower and middle lines on the layout held in place using plaster cloth.

10

More work on the rock faces, which are well over 3.5m long. The greenery is a mixture of static grass fibres and fine foam scatter materials, with coarser foam pieces to represent some bushes and weeds.

11

The scenery above the top track is now receiving attention by first shaping pieces of hard foam. 'Poly Fiber' has been sprayed with hairspray then fine foam scatter material sprinkled on.

12

The rock face made from cork bark, with figures by Bachmann wearing high visibility reflective jackets and trousers for working alongside the track.

Sunrise effect

Johan Leeflang adds interesting lighting effects – and more – to his layout.
Photographs by the author.

As modellers we have to think 'out of the box' to create different effects. After thirty years of dreaming about simulating sunrise and sunset on my layout, I met retired computer programmer Graham Guthrie. He made an electronic micro-processor module which controls the timing and light intensity of the 40watt coloured lamps which create the lighting effects behind a mountain backdrop photograph.

Installing the lights

The first step was to split the backscene into two separate backdrops, a mountain scene in front of a cloudy sky. The sky is a Masonite board curved at the ceiling, painted sky blue. The clouds were painted on by an artist.
With the help of my friend and fellow model enthusiast Hans Bac, I installed a row of coloured lamps below the backdrops in the 150mm space between them. There is a yellow lamp in the centre, mounted higher on a metal rod, closer to the horizon of the mountain backdrop, to simulate the sun.
On either side it is flanked by an orange, a red, and two blue lamps. Between the coloured lamps are eight equally spaced white lights.

1. Blue lights on

The dimly lit blue lights softly illuminate the sky above the sleeping layout.
To enhance the night time effect, blue and green lights were installed on the ceiling behind the valance, with a ratio of two blue to one green. These are controlled by dimmers to regulate the desired effect. This is important because at night not everything outside is totally dark so with this lighting there is always a little light on the layout, not just lights through the windows of buildings or rolling stock going past.
Pink clouds are the first signs of dawn.
While the blue lights remain on, the red lights come on and slowly get brighter.

2. Red lights starting

3. Red lights on, orange starting

Slowly the reds change to orange as the sky brightens up.
The blue lights are still dimly lit and the red lights are getting brighter as the orange lights come on and also gradually get brighter.

4. Orange on, yellow starting

5. Yellow on, white starting

Reds and oranges brighten to yellow as dawn breaks and sunrise is imminent.
The yellow light is switched on to add its colour and brightness to the clouds and sky as the other coloured lights start to fade.

6. White light on

7. Full daylight

Although the mountains are still in silhouette, bright white daylight floods the sky as the sun rises. The white lights quickly brighten as all the other coloured lights are faded and switched off. Finally, the mountains are visible in all their splendour as the whole model railway lights up and comes to life. The main lighting, together with the white lights behind the mountain, illuminate the layout.
Although it is all over in less than a minute, the sunrise is amazingly realistic. Sunset is simply a reversal of the sunrise lighting sequence.

Mist over the mountains

The idea of simulating mist over the mountain scenery came about after visiting Switzerland in 2007. Whilst travelling by train over the Albula mountain range, thick mist appeared before entering the Albula tunnel at Preda.

8. Mist

At a local music shop a fog machine was purchased, the type used in stage productions and at discos. A thick metal pipe was placed over the machine's outlet. Small holes were drilled along the top of the first part of this pipe, then slightly larger holes towards the end. When the machine warms up (which takes a few minutes), the mist rolls over the mountain backdrop and drops down to just above track level.

I may have been lucky with the flow of air in the layout room. It might be necessary to install a few small computer fans in hidden spots to give the mist 'movement'. The fog will disappear after a while.

A very theatrical effect is achieved when the mist and lighting is used simultaneously.

The sky at night

The moon and stars can be achieved by using an 'invisible ink' ultra-violet marker pen, as used for security marking. The moon and a lot of small dots drawn on the sky background will not be seen under normal lighting but can be revealed by an ultra-violet light behind the valance.

***Editor's note**: past experience suggests that theatrical fog or smoke machines like that used here may leave a deposit which could affect the cleanliness of the track and scenery.*

Care should also be taken if the premises are fitted with smoke alarms.